Also by WR Peden

Tripton-Z Series:
Book 1: Soldiers of ZED
Book 2: Aftermath (Coming Soon)

Adult Grayscale Coloring Books:
Hot Rod Heaven

NWA Ringside Magazine:
September 2014
November 2014
January 2015
Feburary 2015
May 2015

Check out other books by WR Peden online at
www.HawkstarEnt.com/wr-peden

Hot Rod Heaven

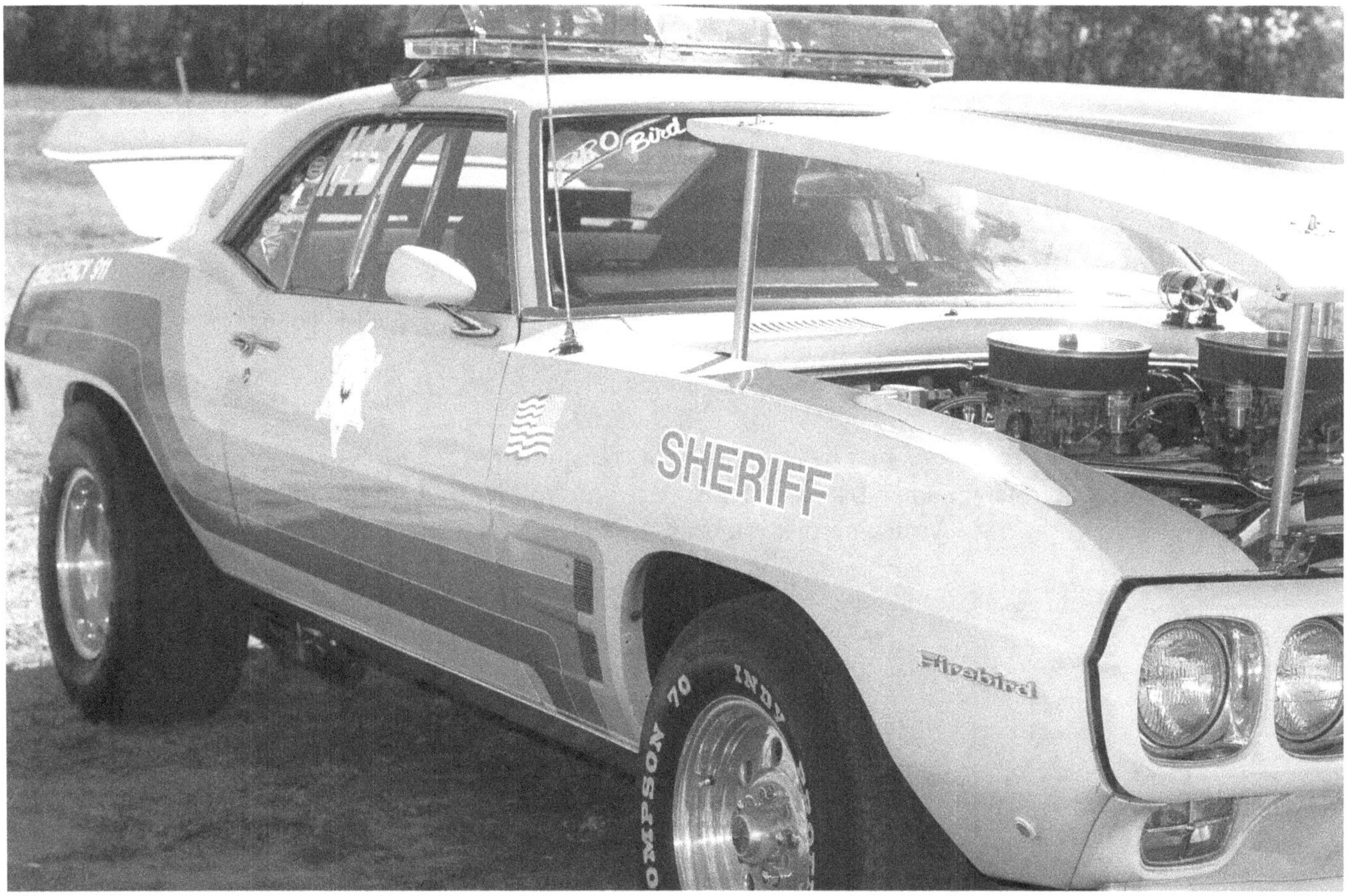

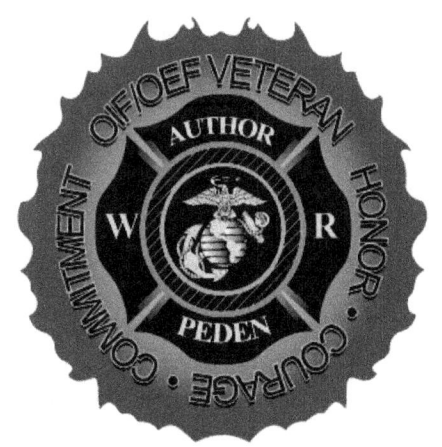

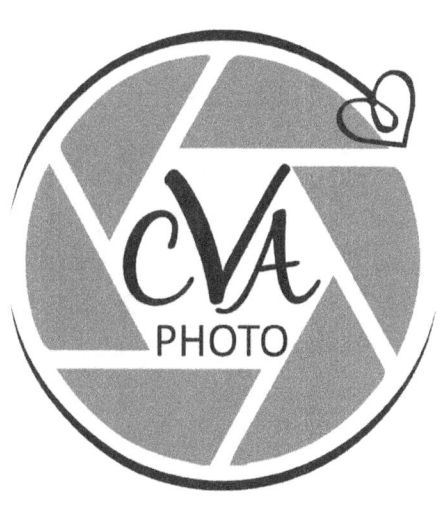

First Published 2017

Copyright © 2017 WR Peden
Images Copyright © 2017 CVA Photo
Design Copyright © 2017 Will Designs

www.Hawkstarent.com/WR-Peden
www.CVAPhotoStudio.com

All rights reserved. No part of this book may be reproduced or transmitted in any form or by any means, including but not limited to information storage and retrieval systems, electronic, mechanical, photocopy, recording, etc. without written permission from the copyright holders.

Images used under license from CVA Photo and CVAPhotoStudio.com

ISBN-13: 978-1979225359
ISBN-10: 1979225354

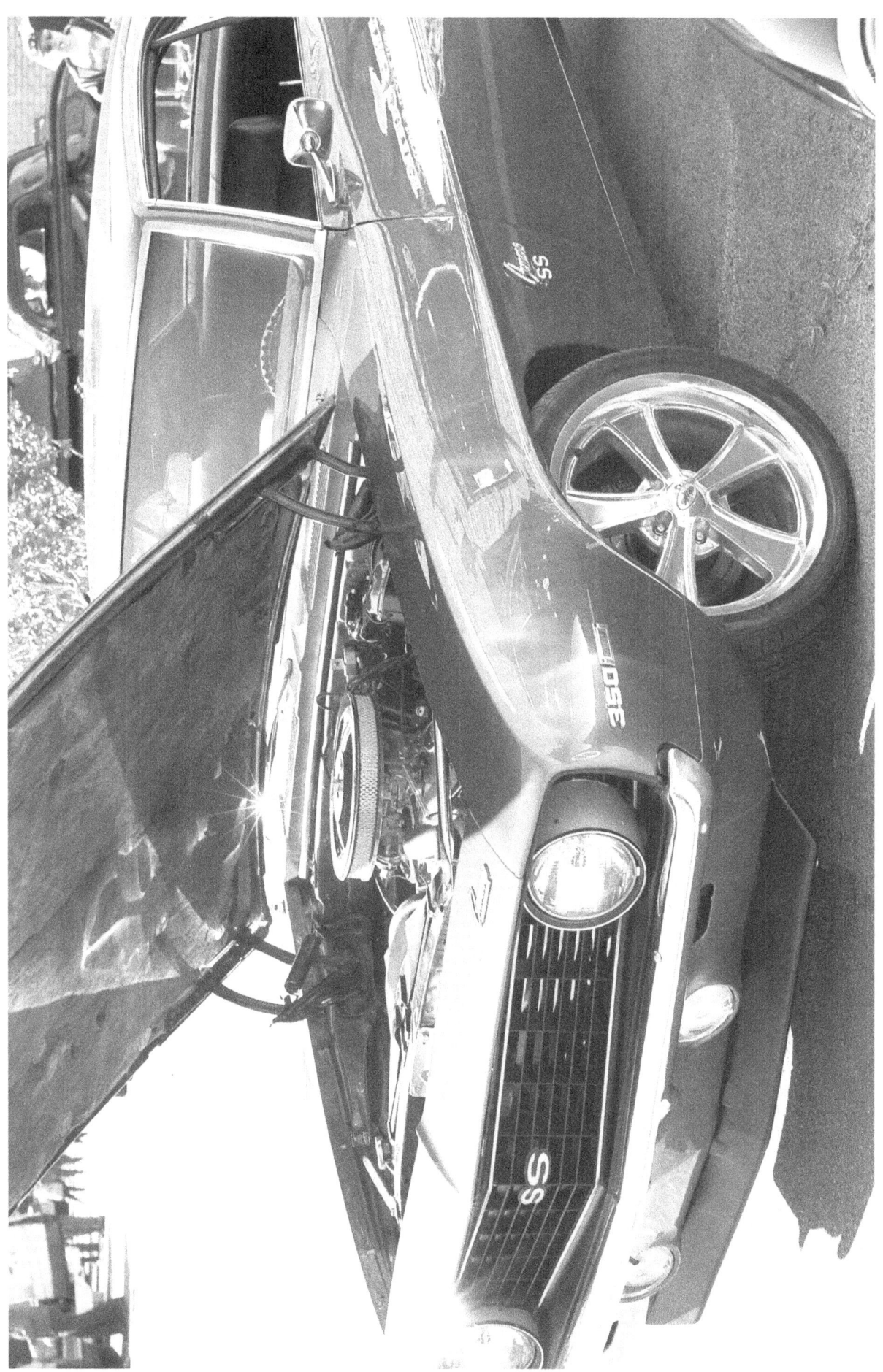

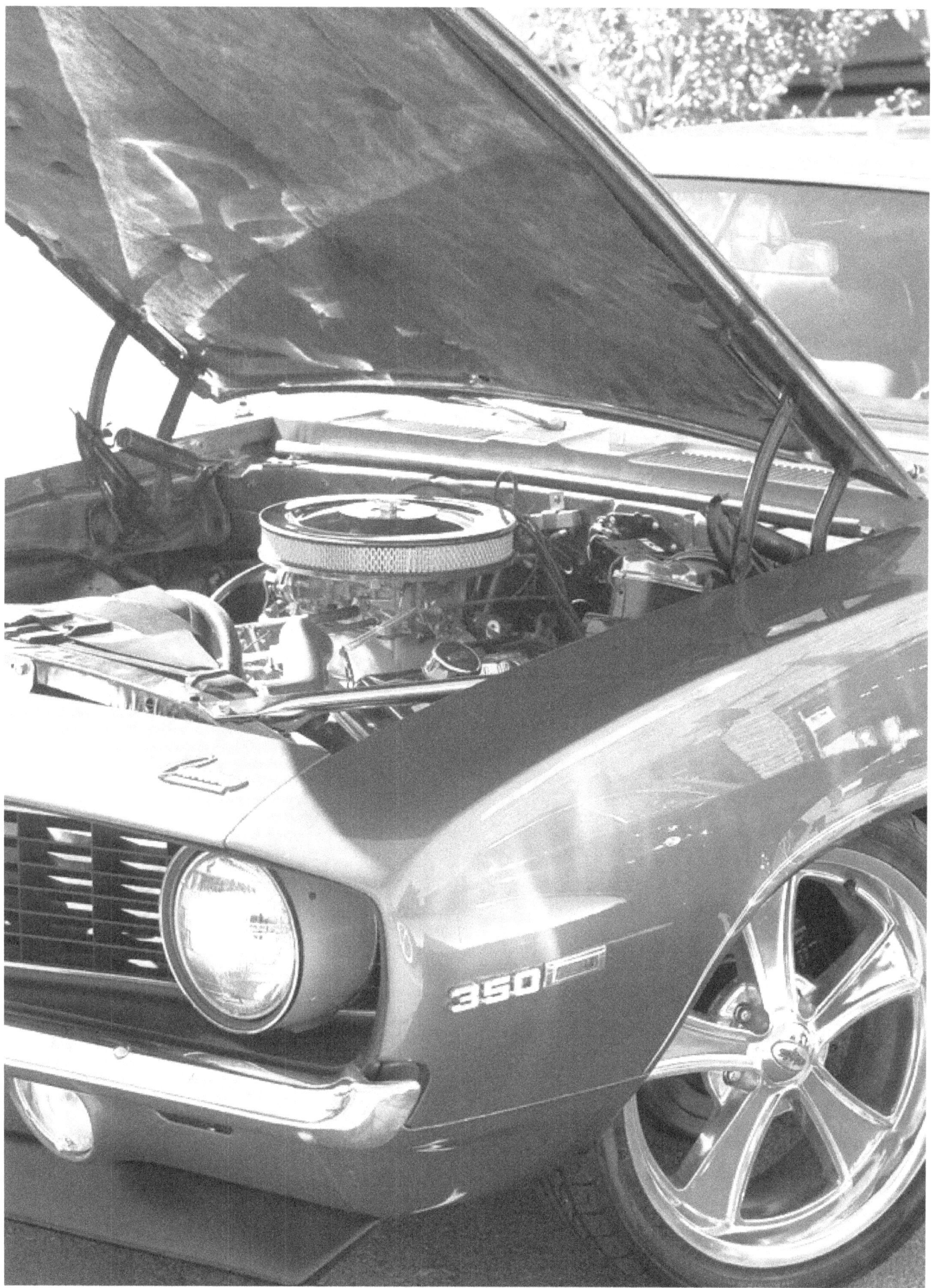

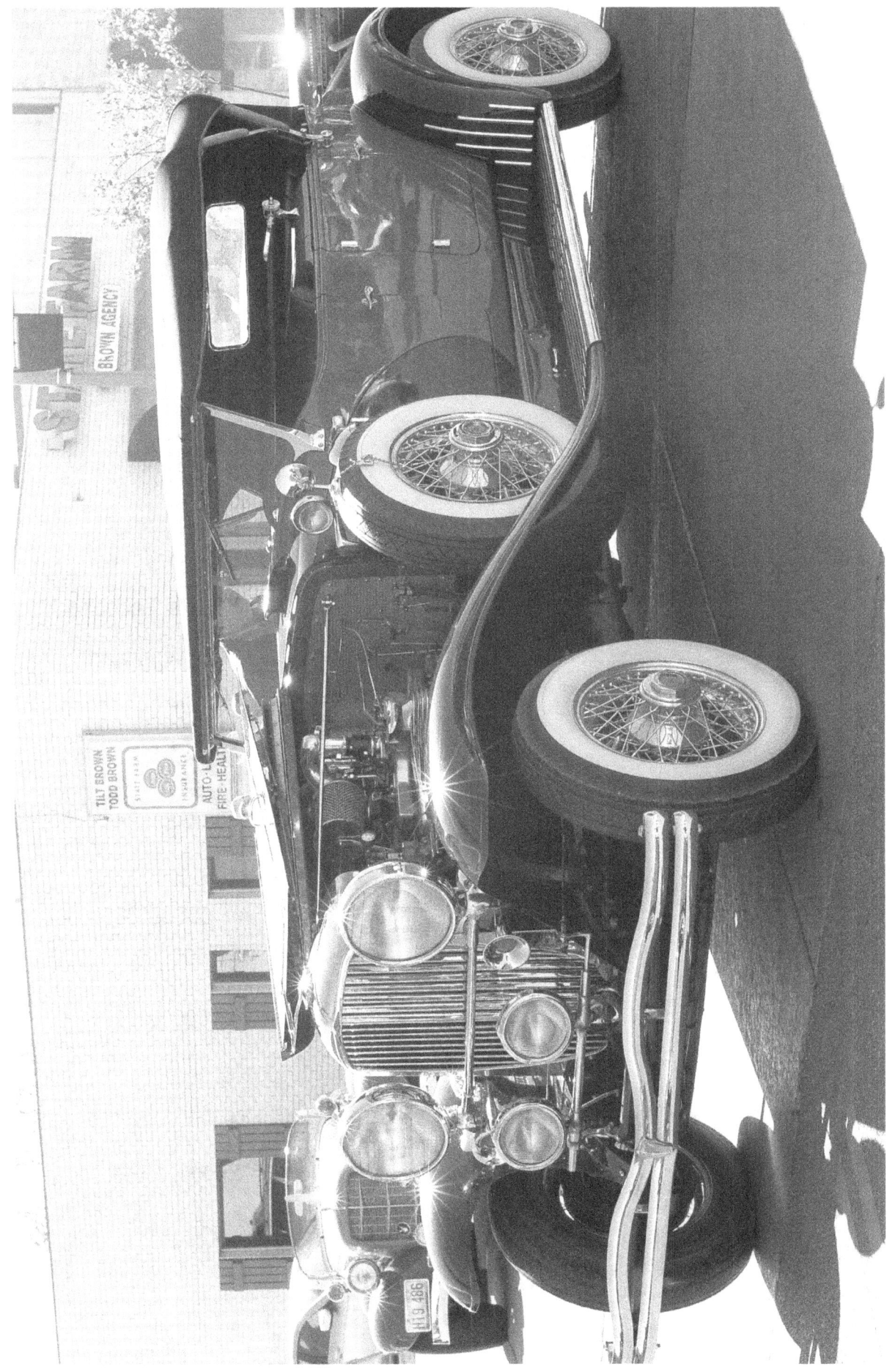

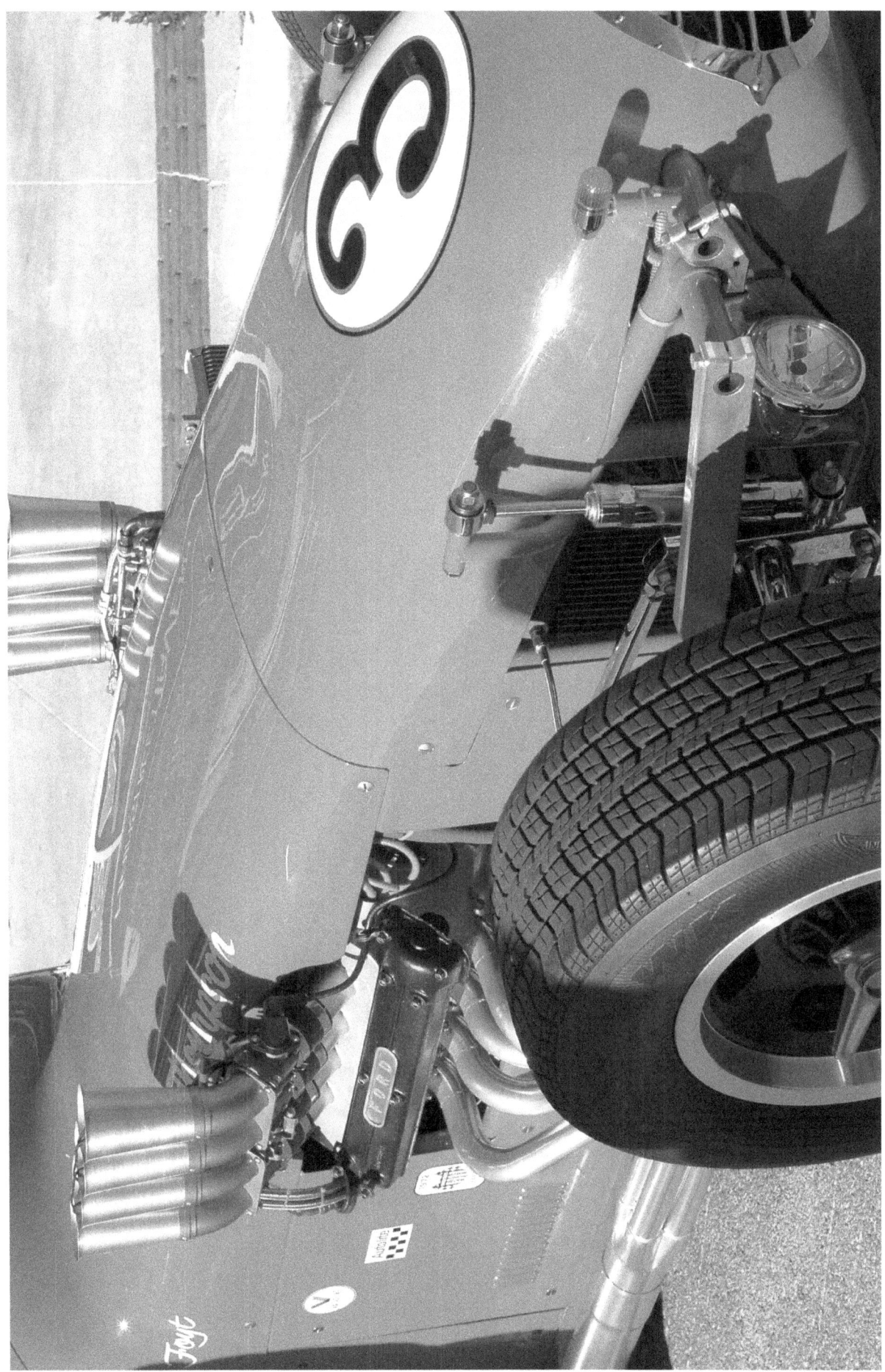

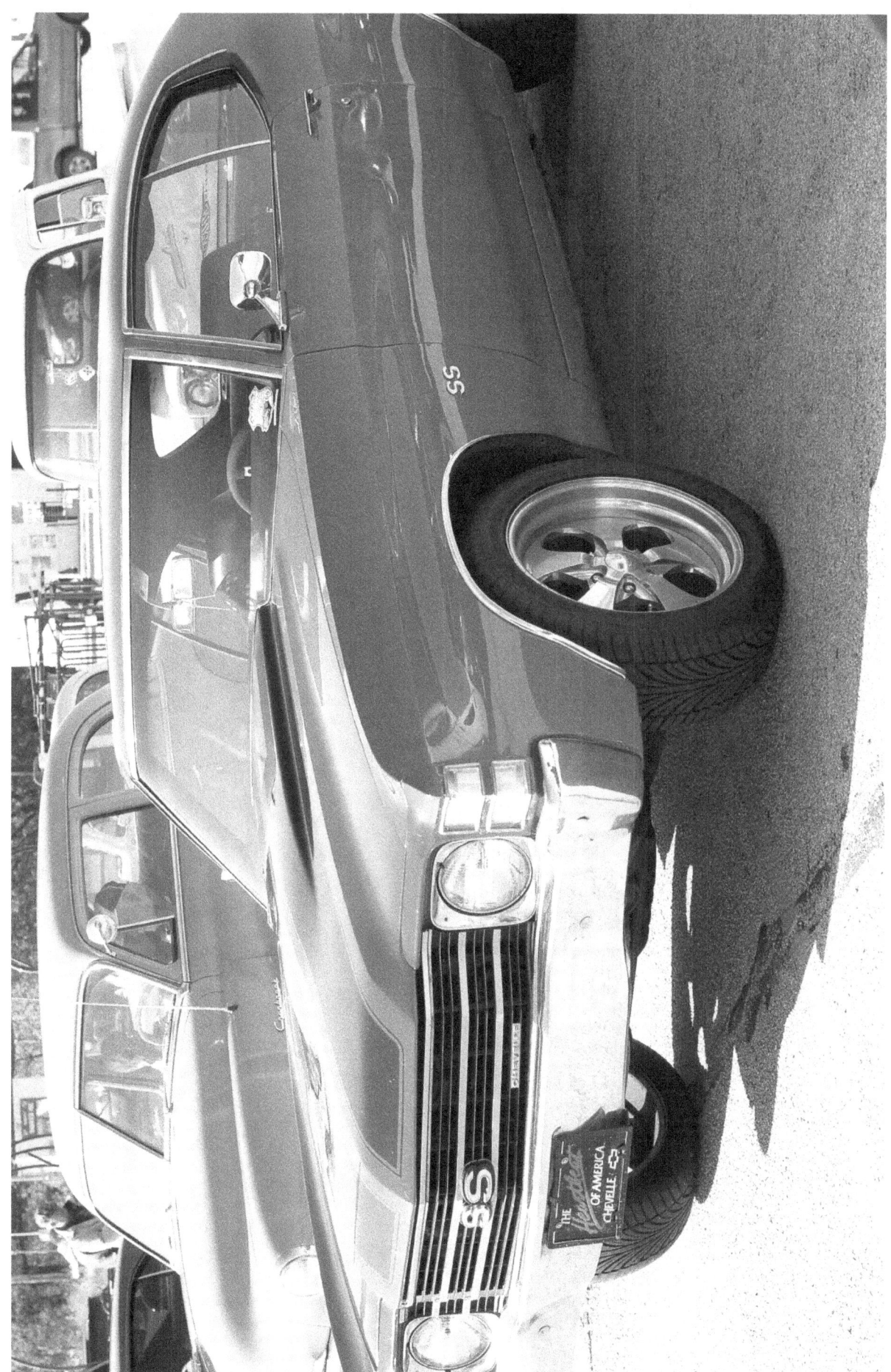

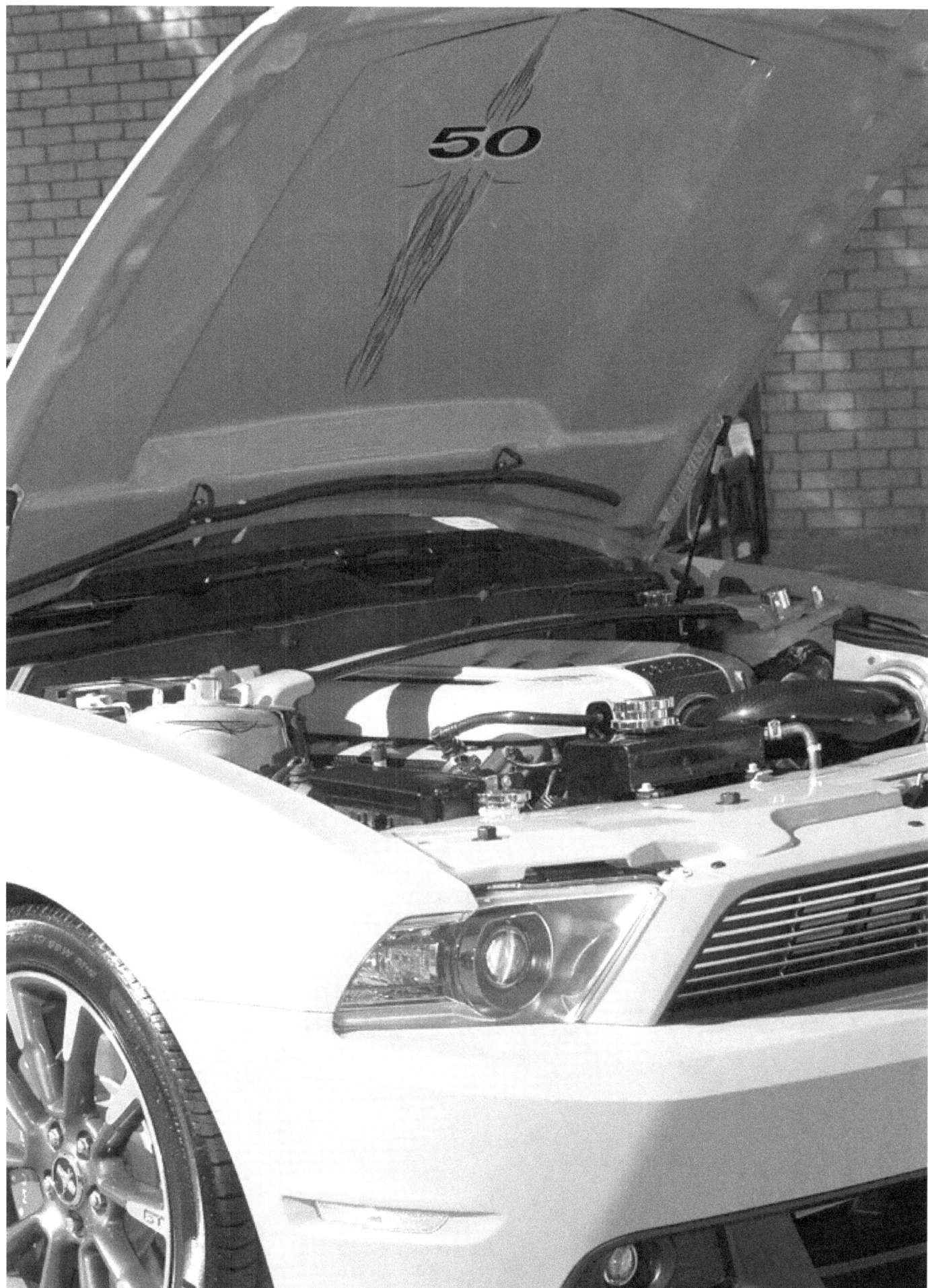

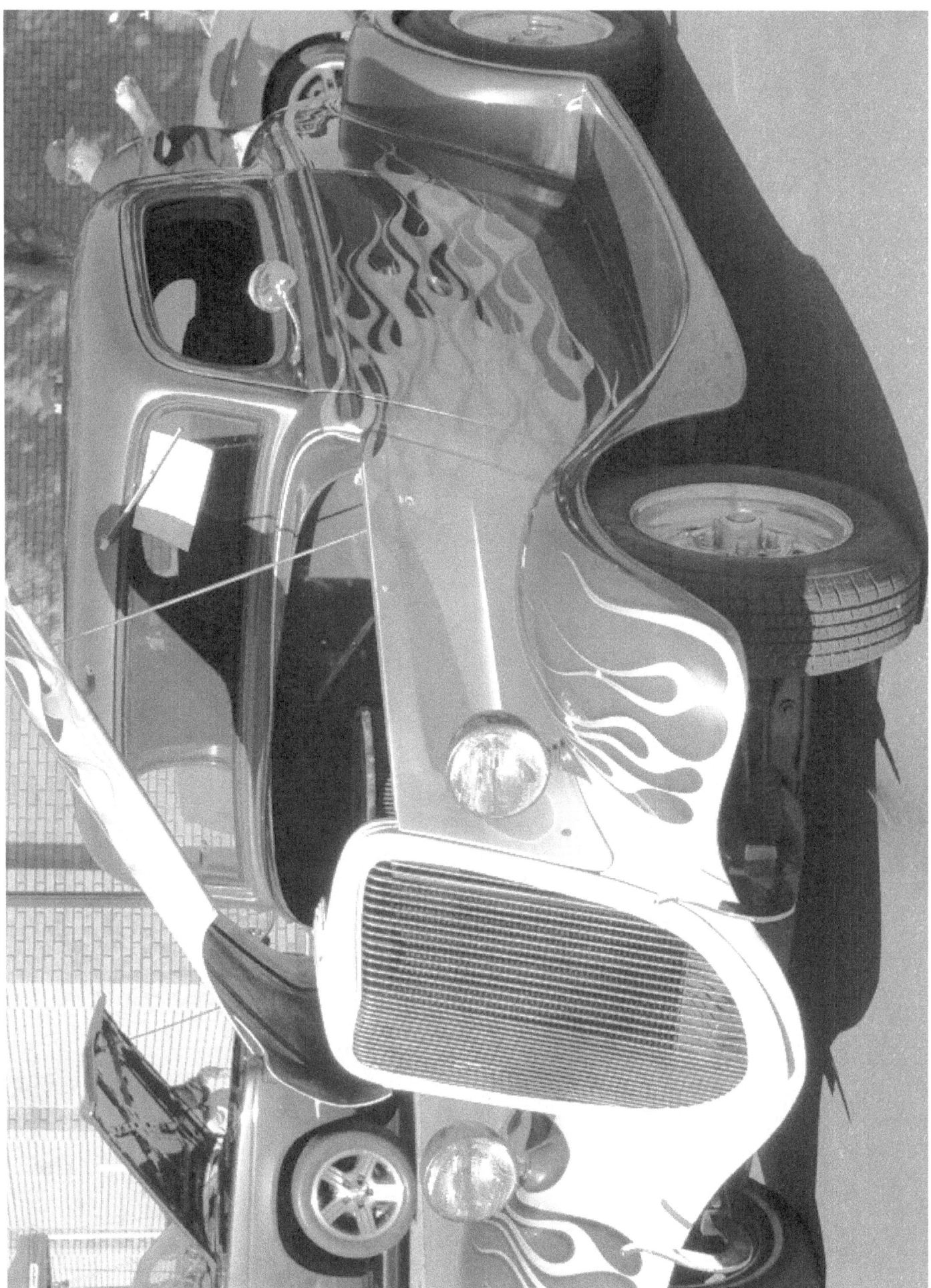

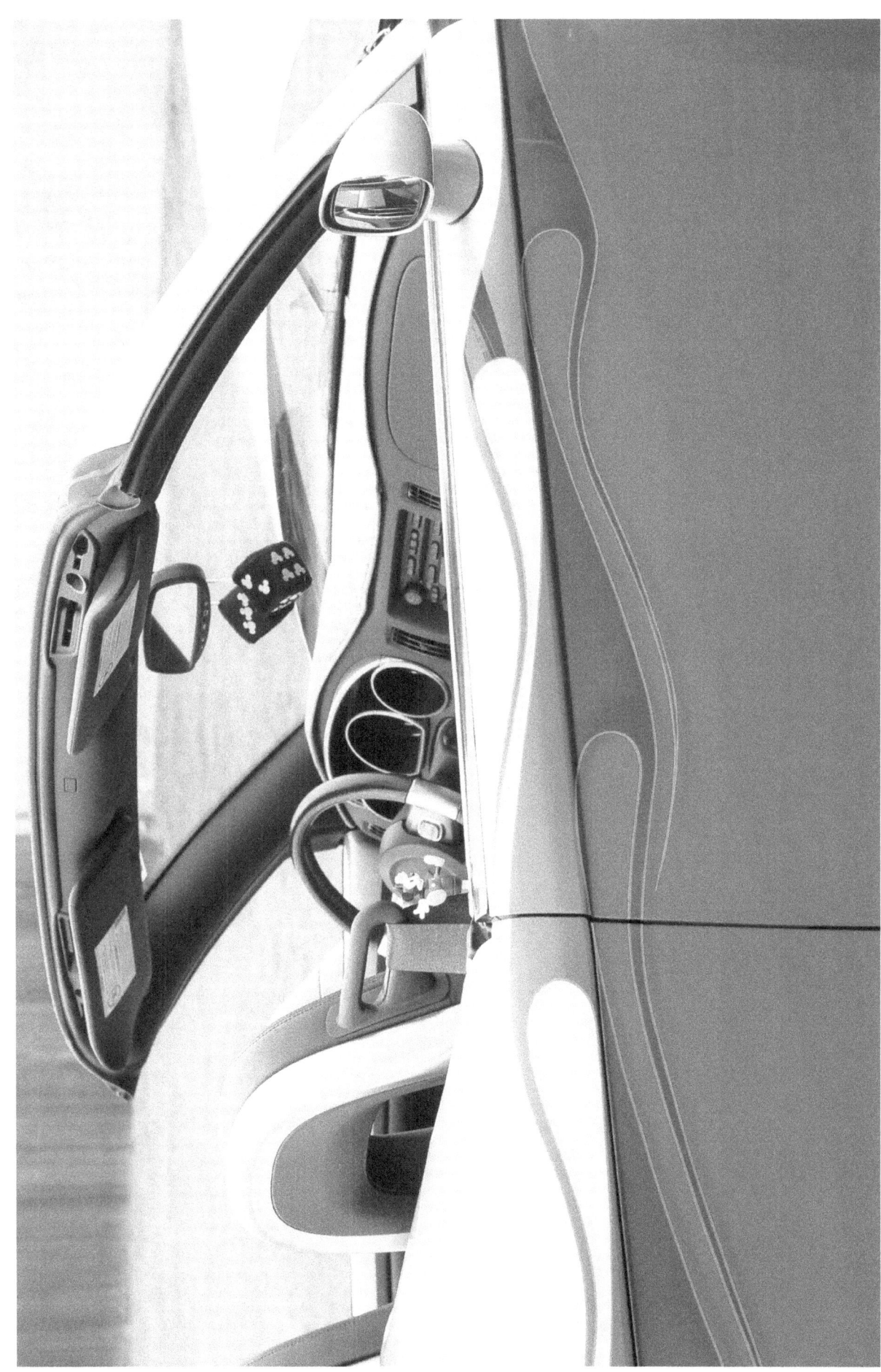

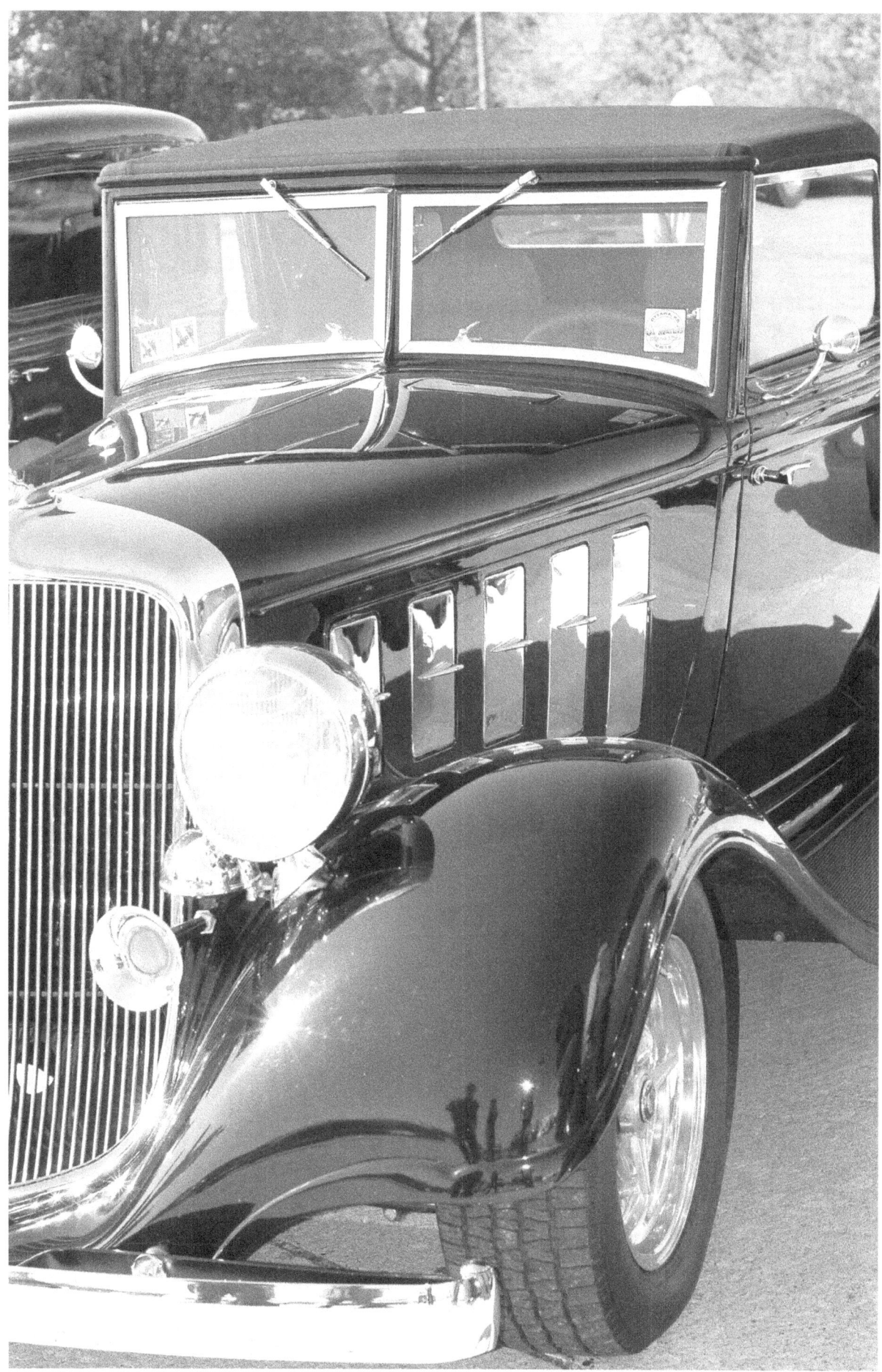

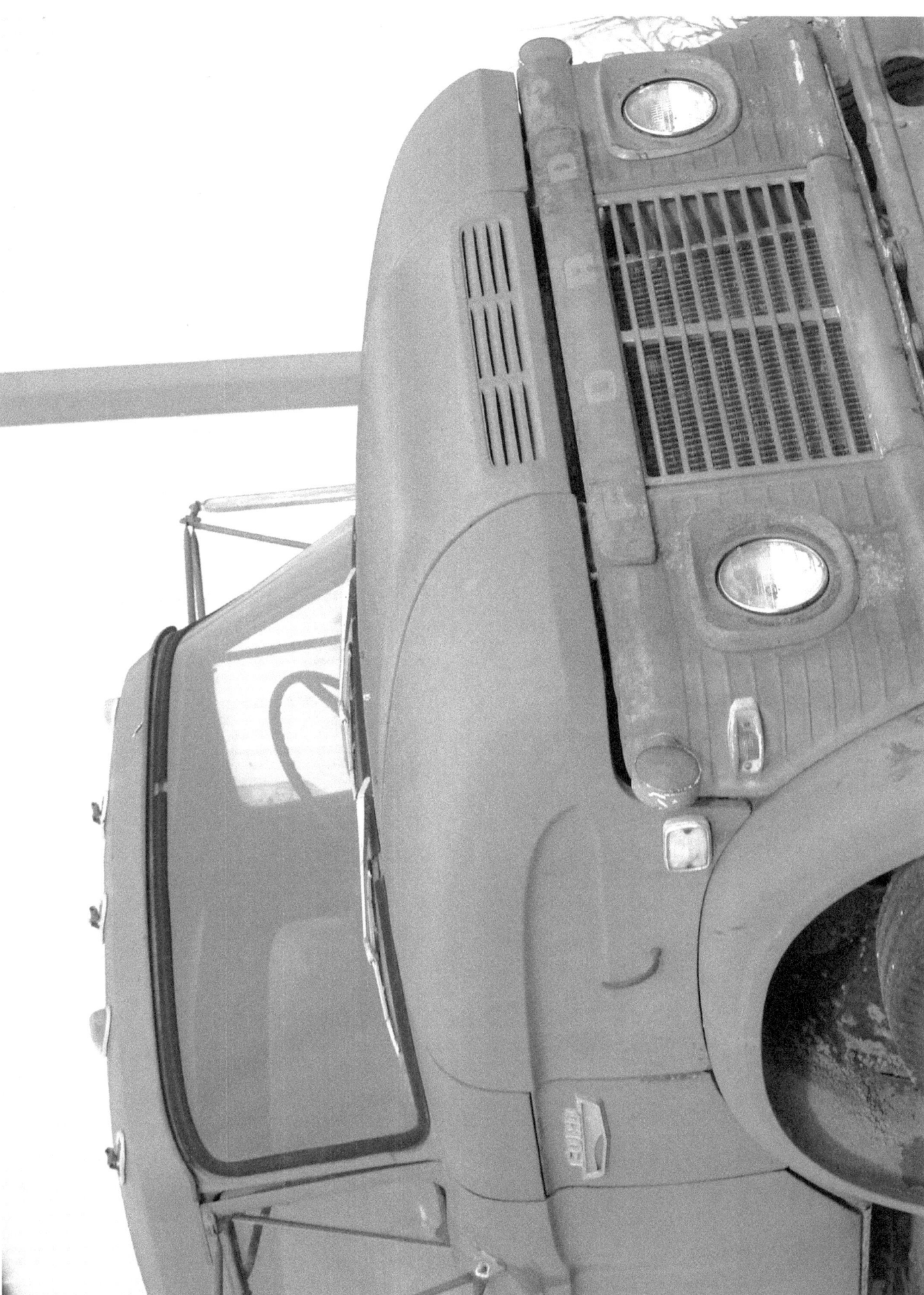

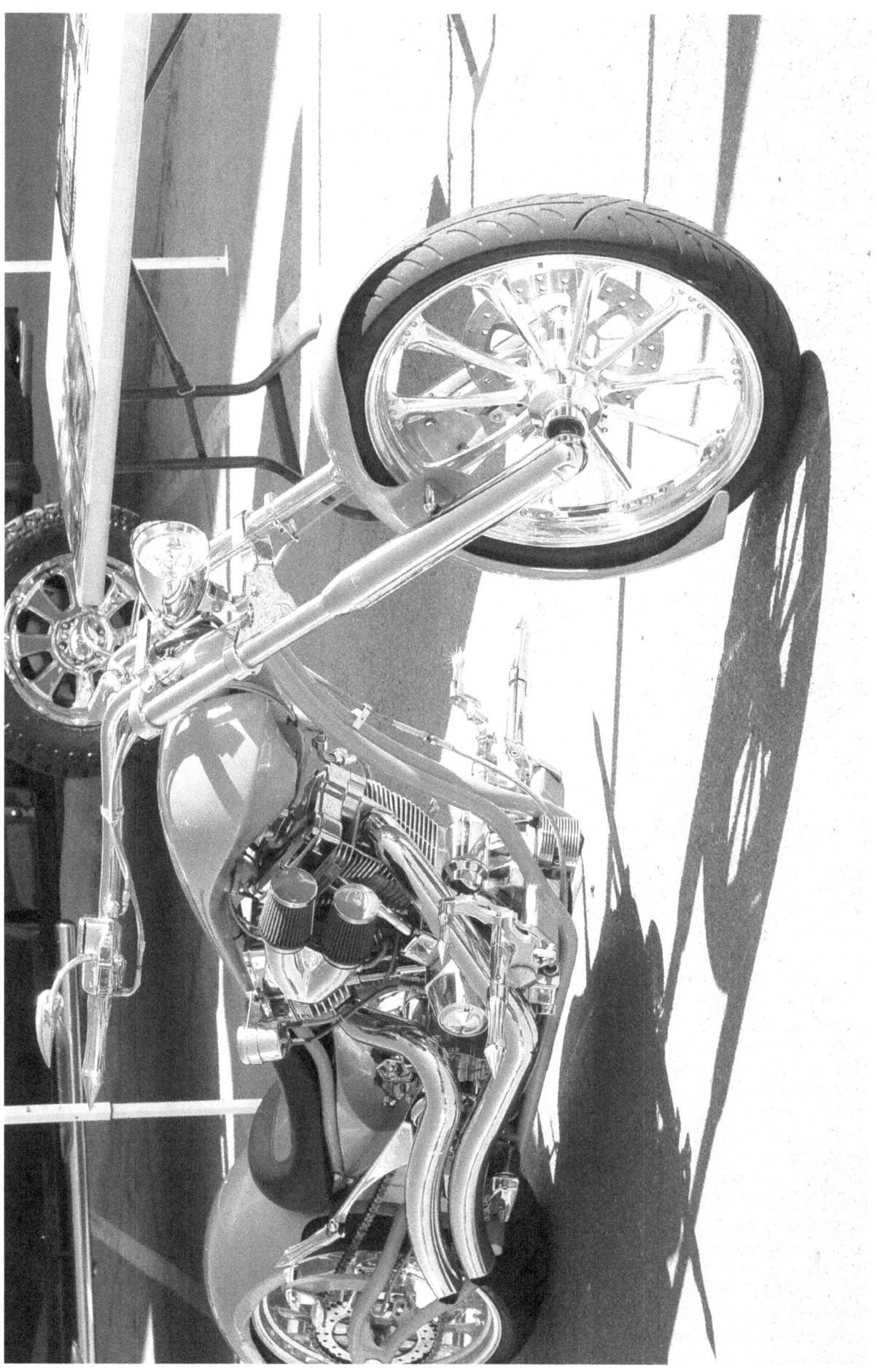

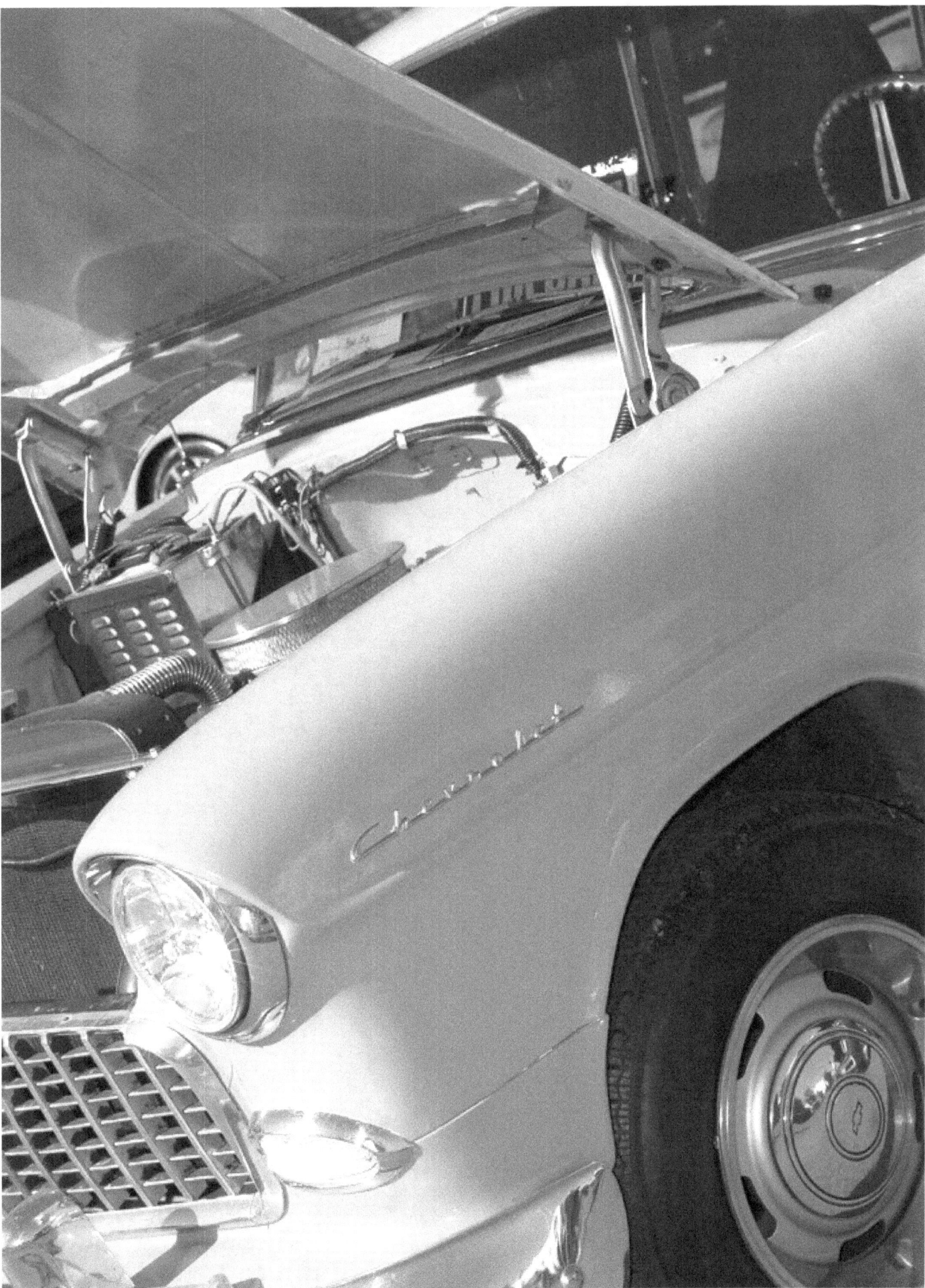

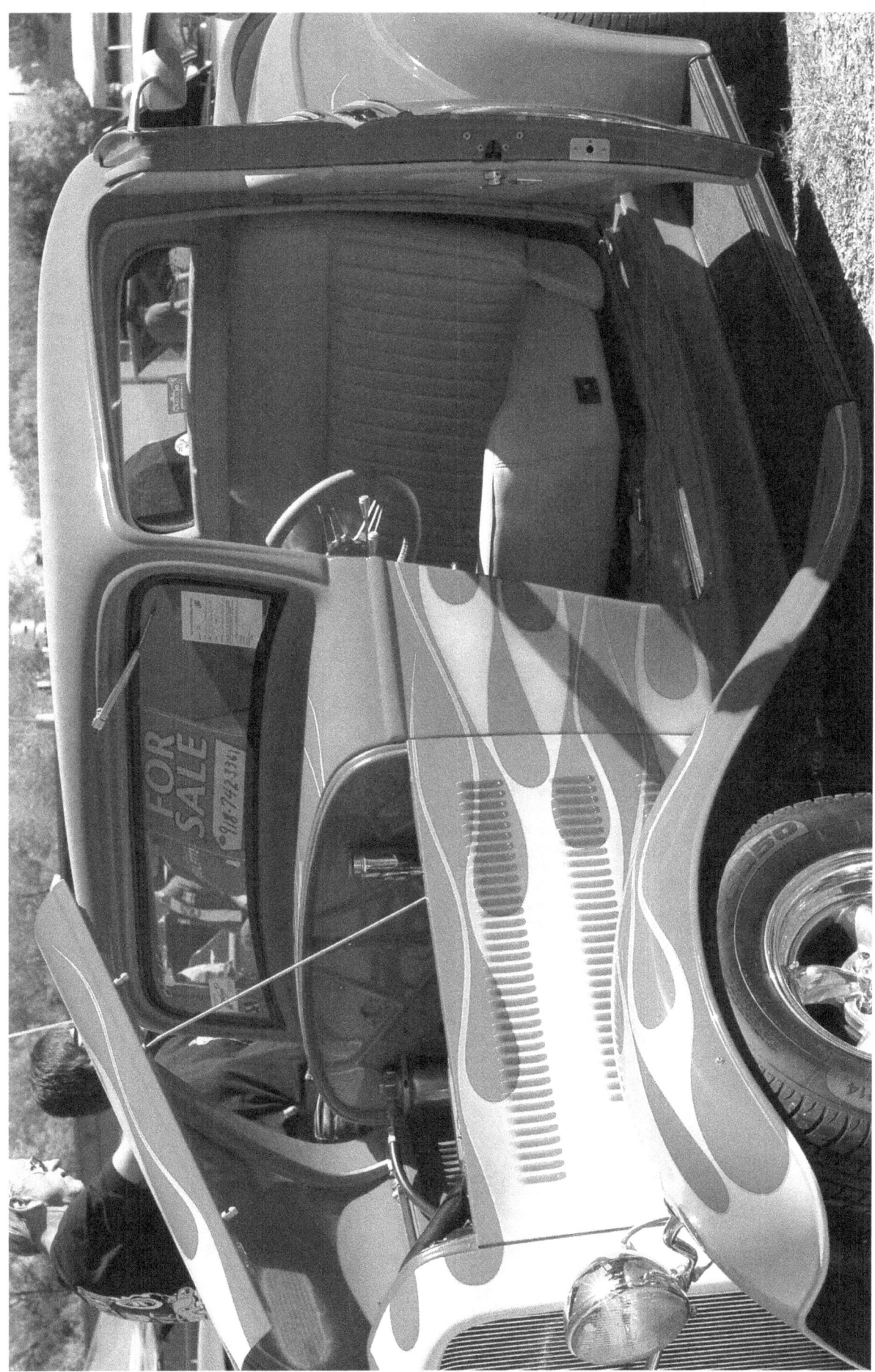

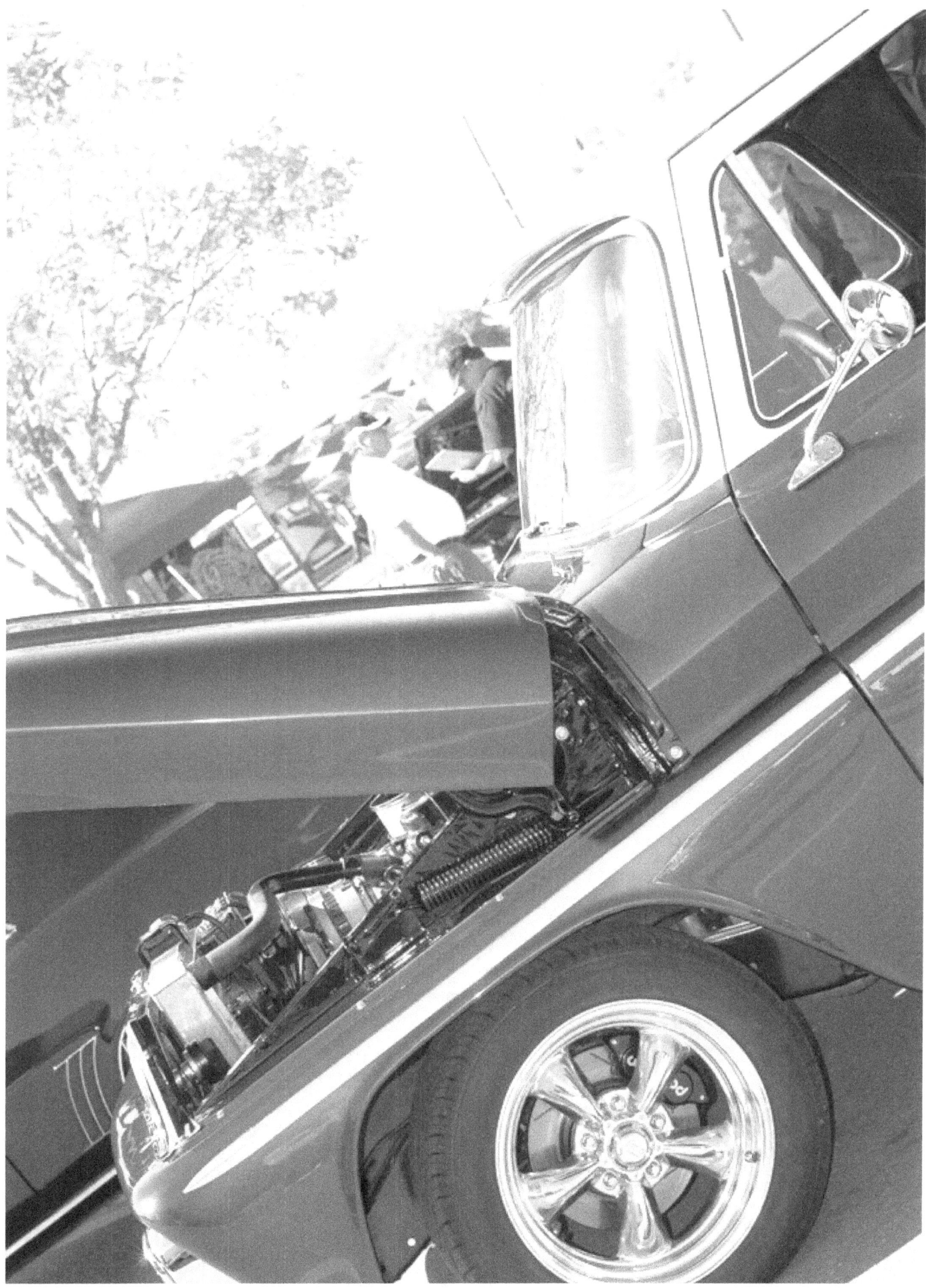

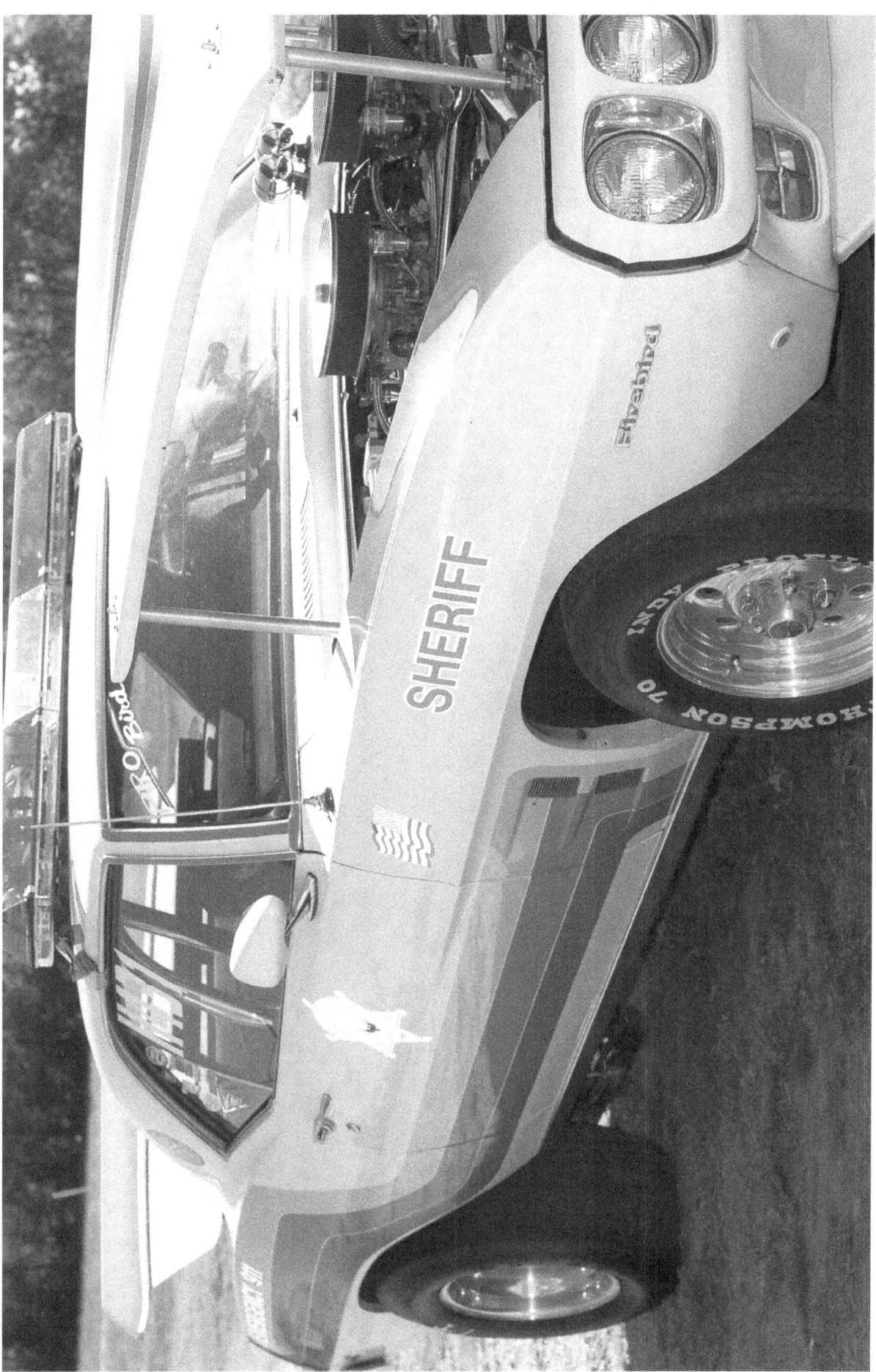

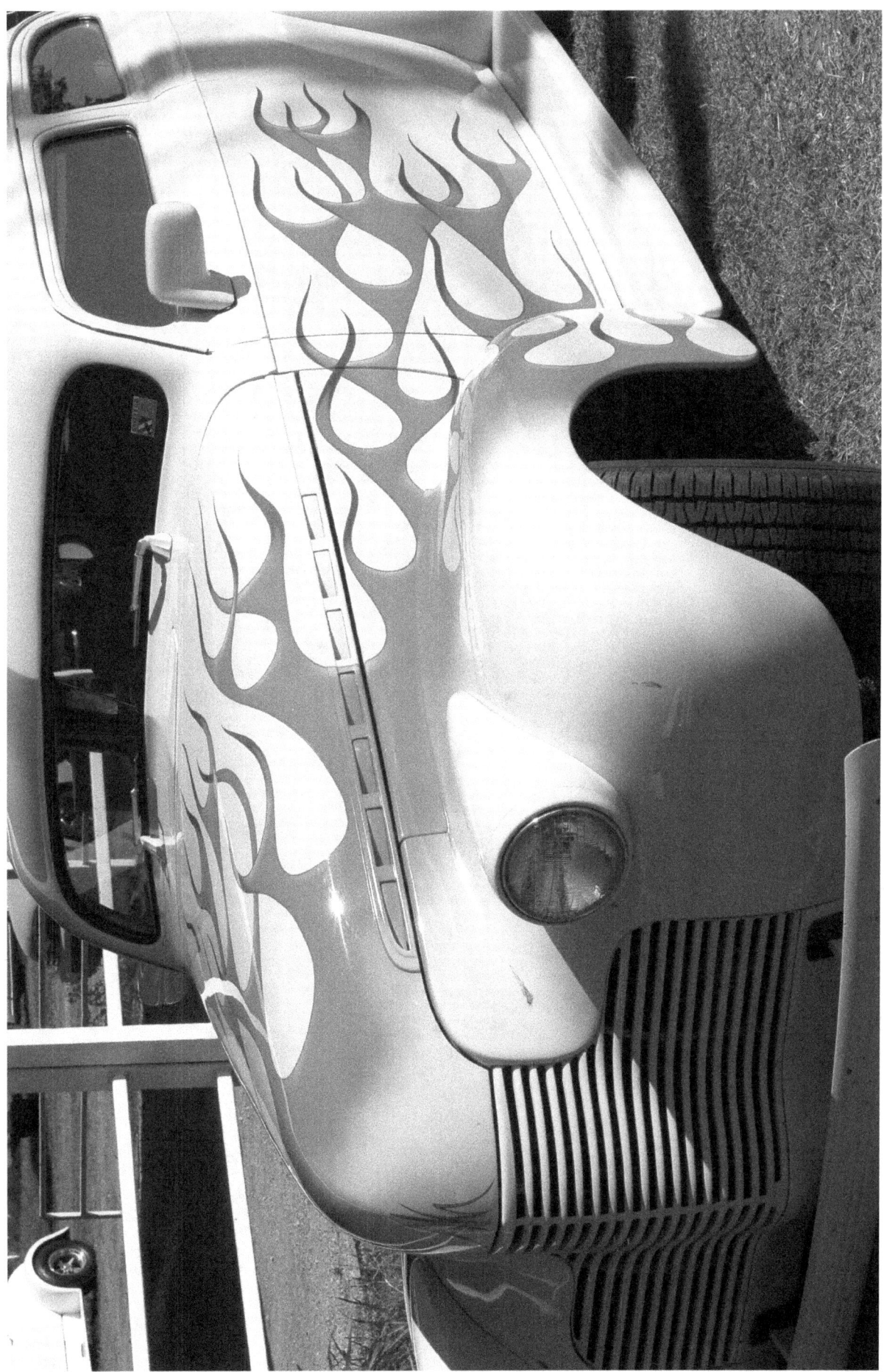

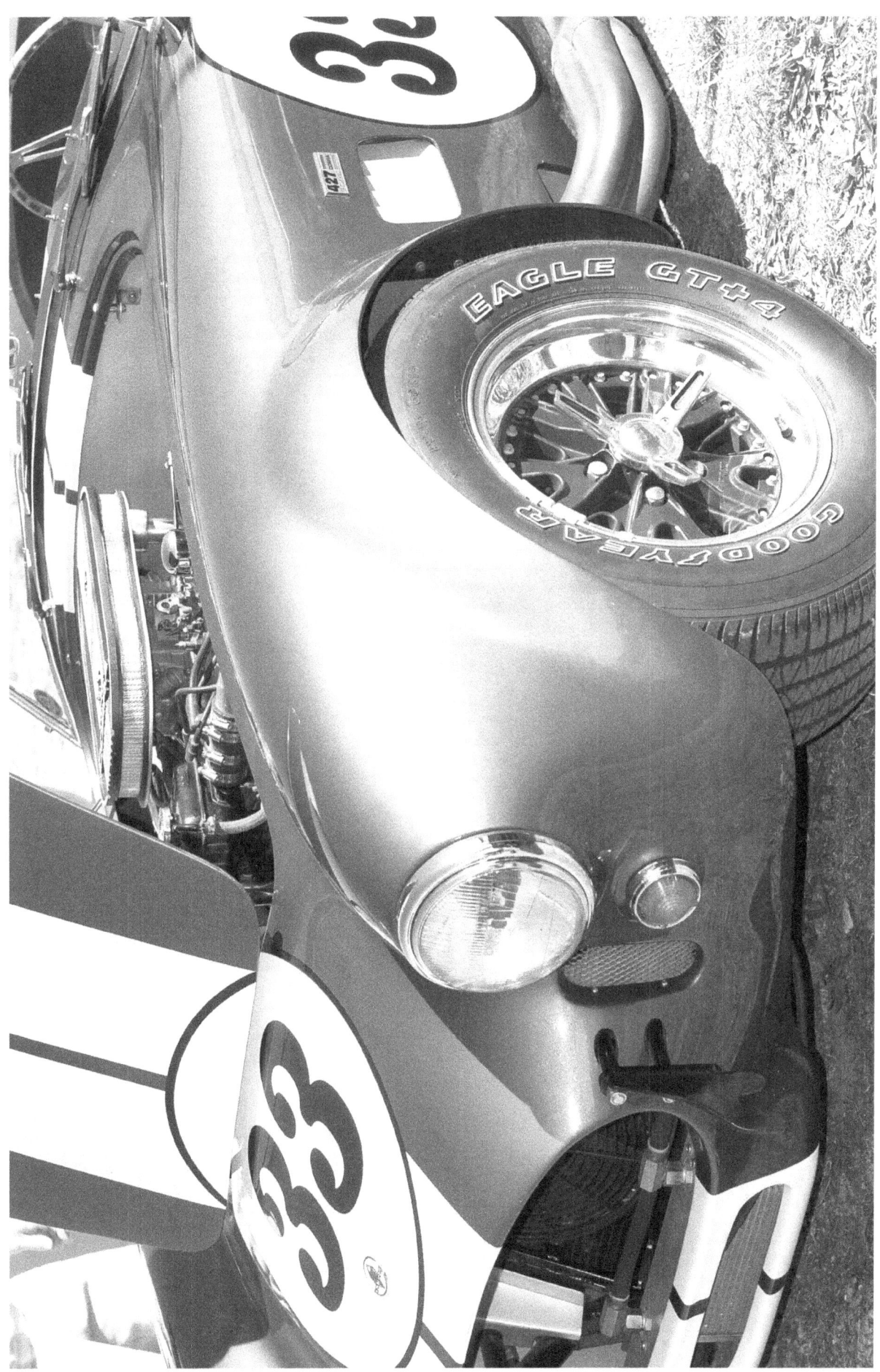

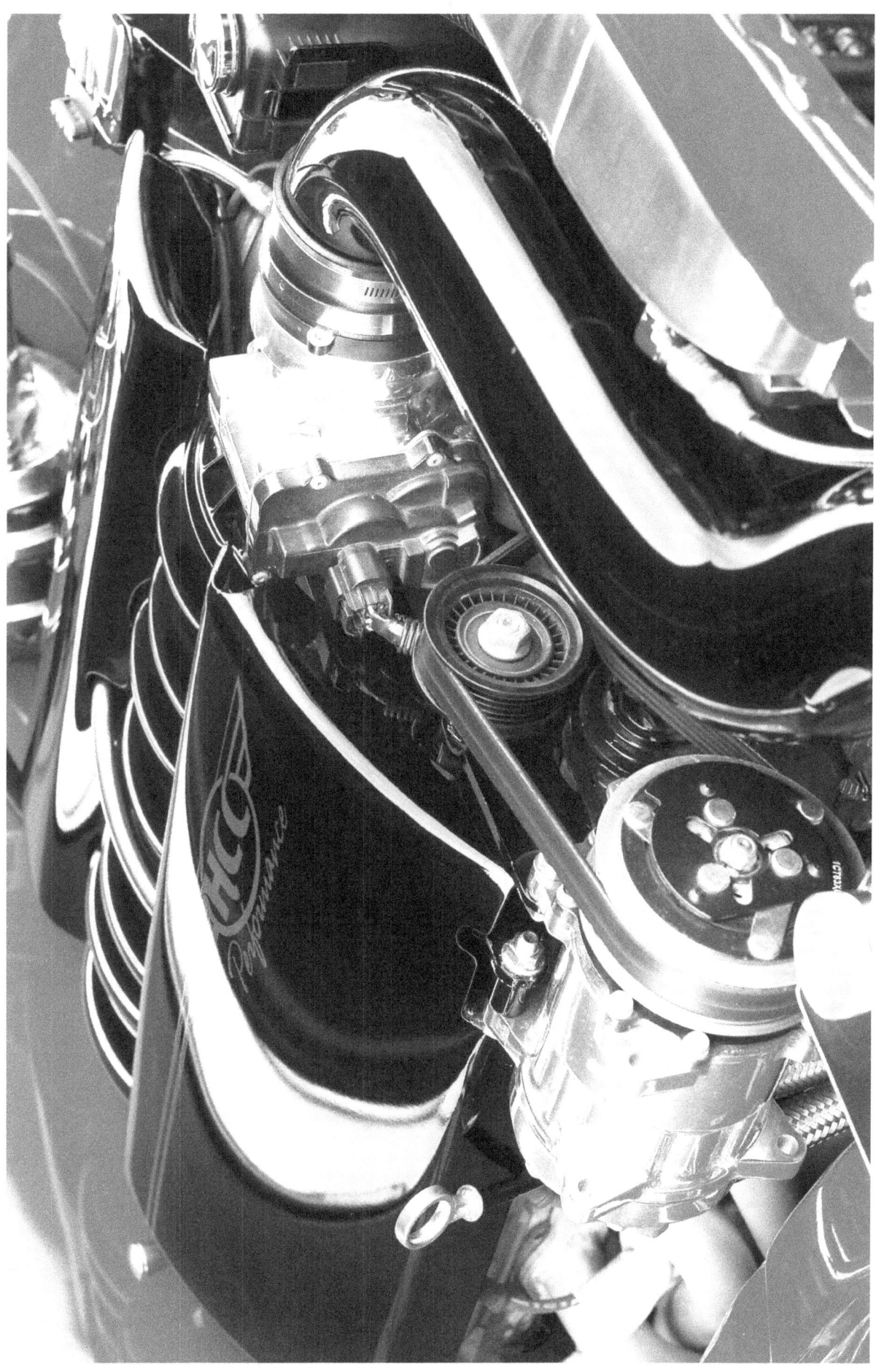

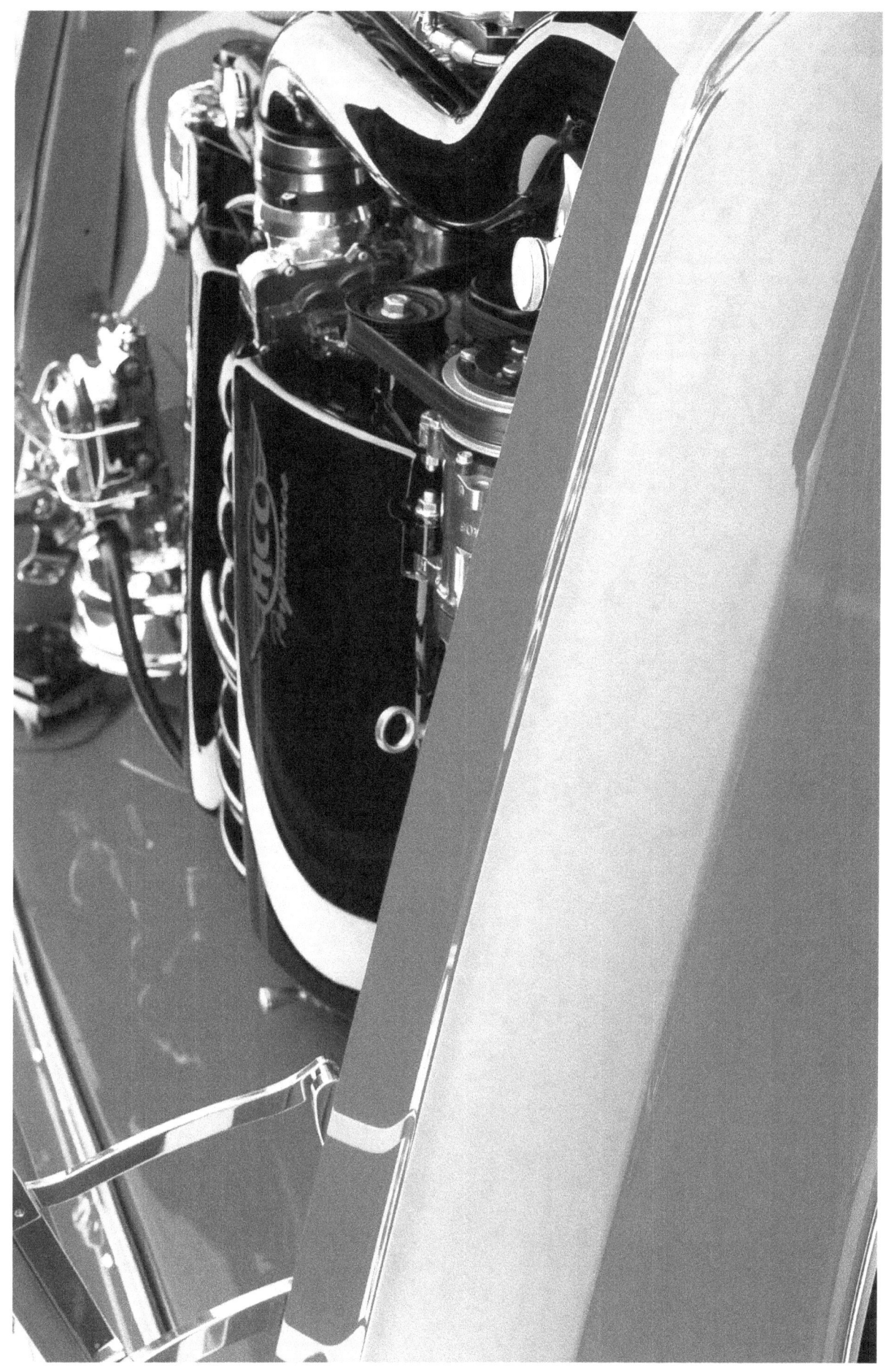

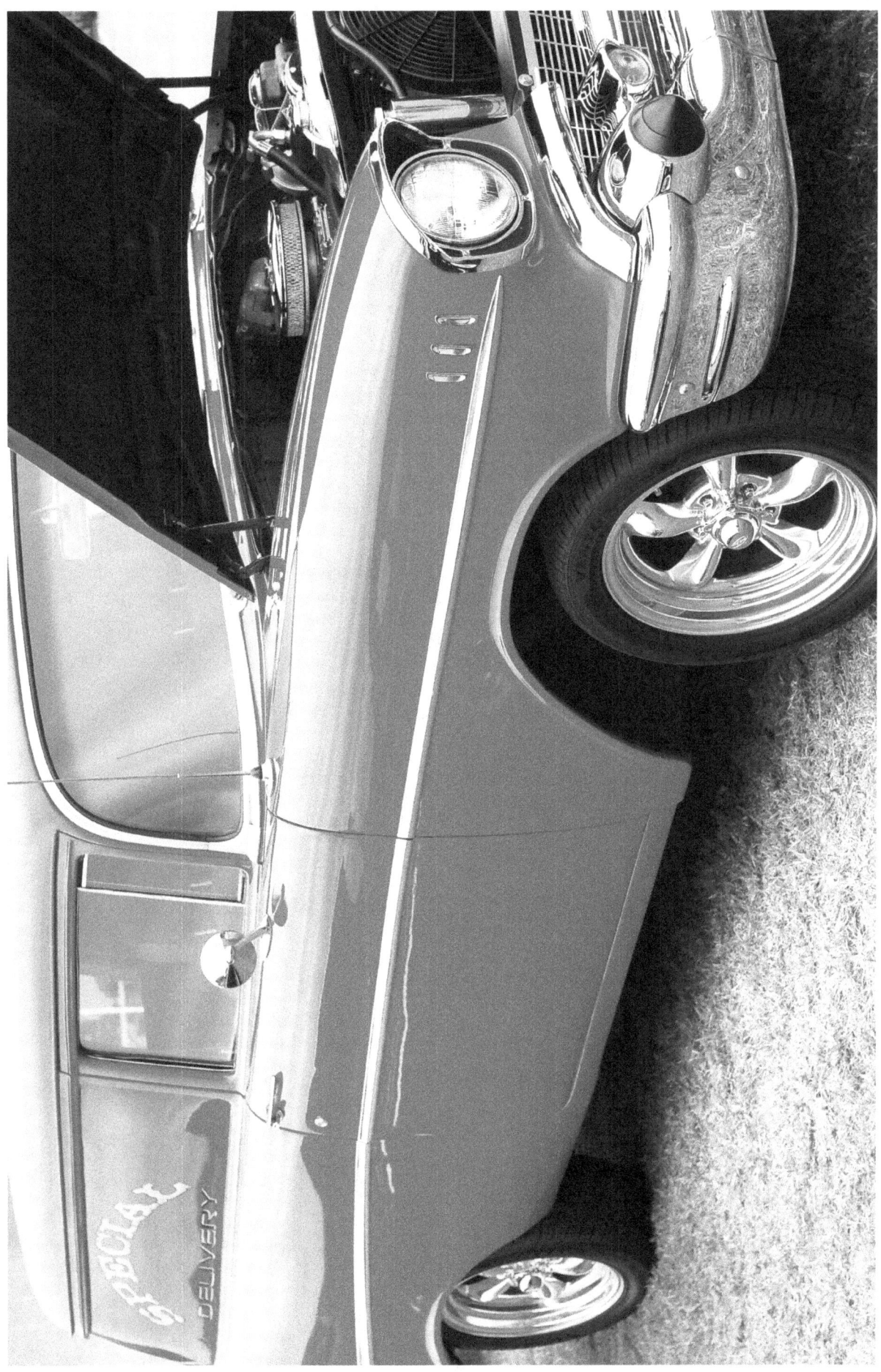

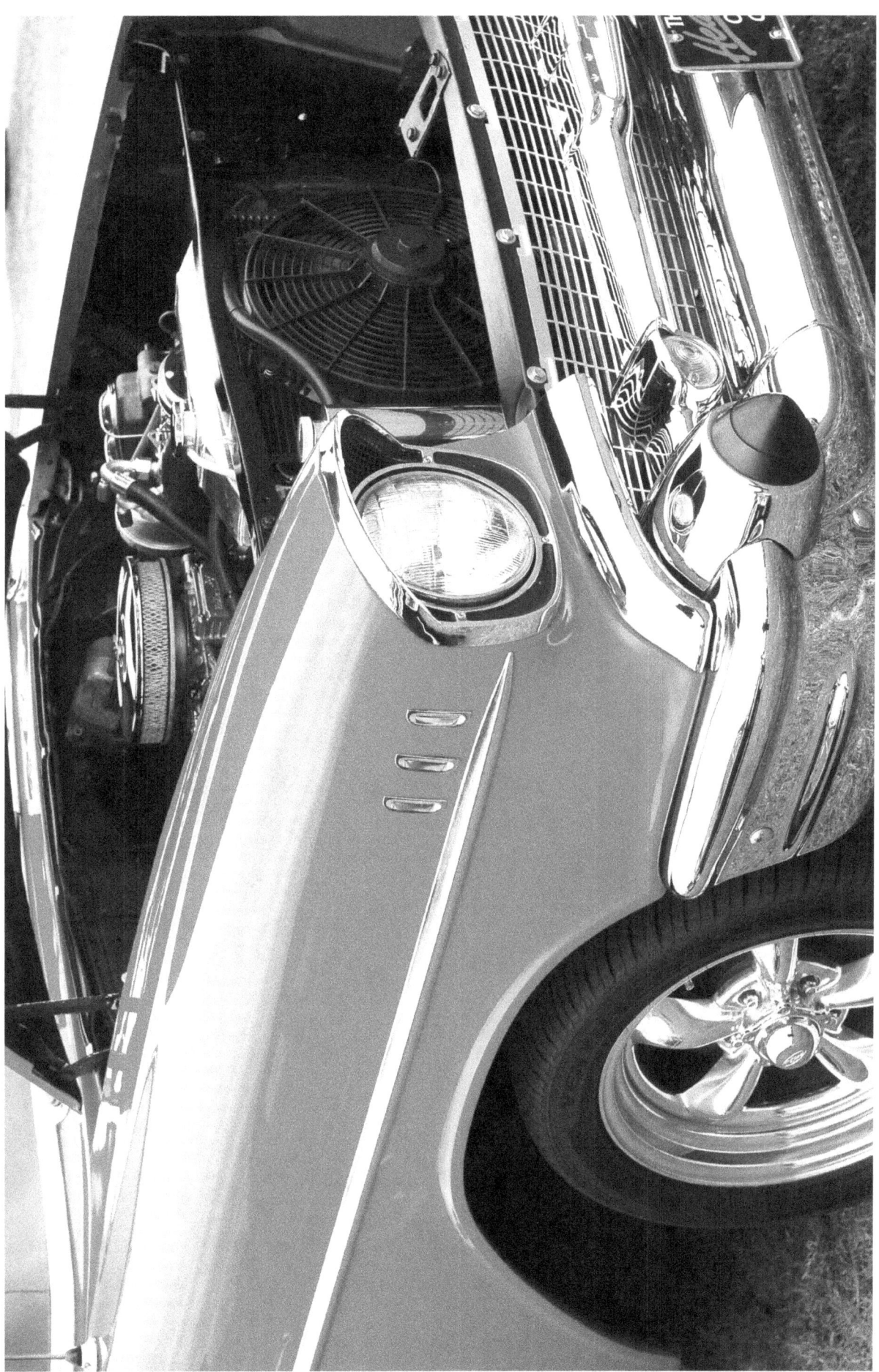

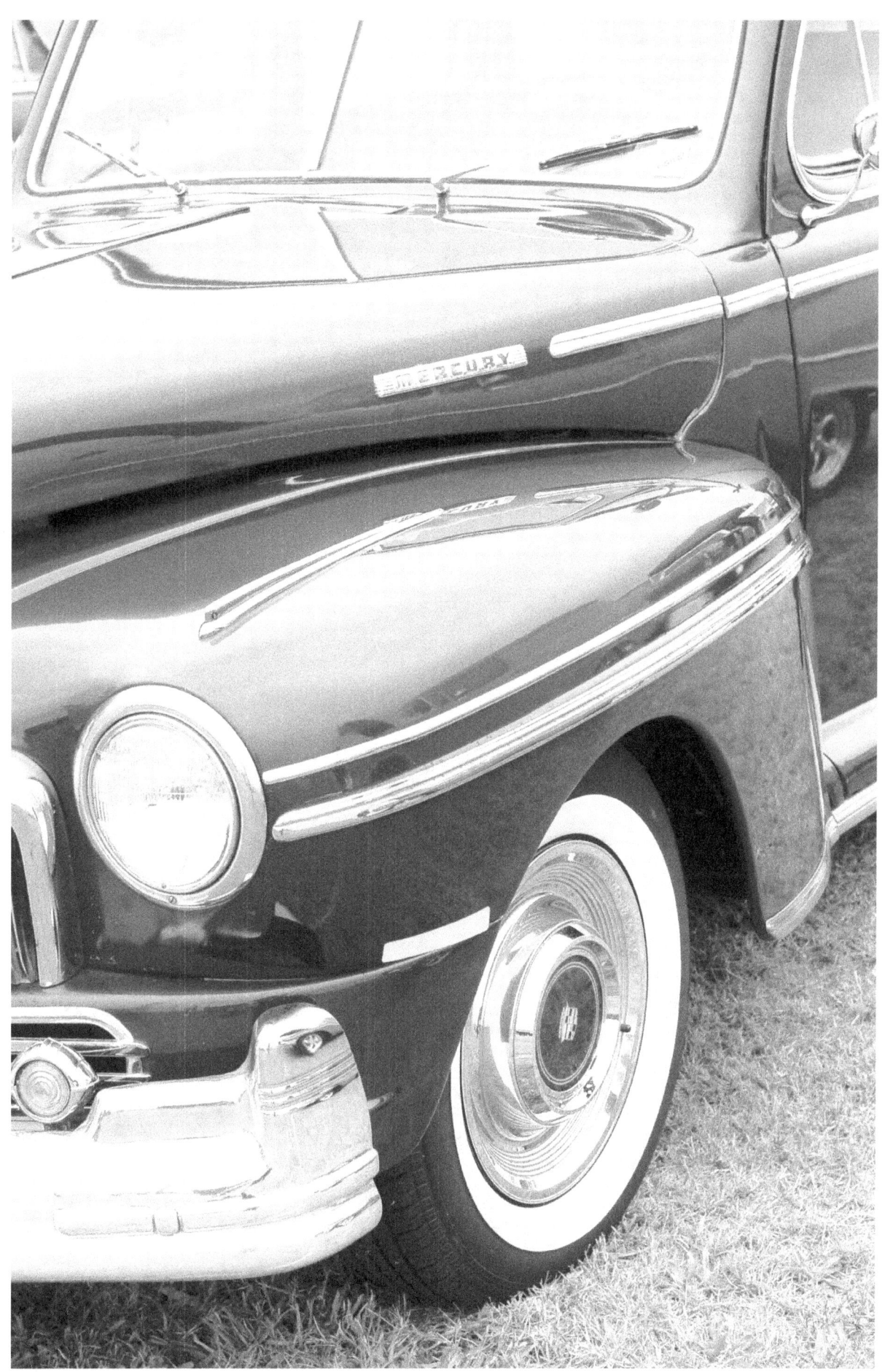

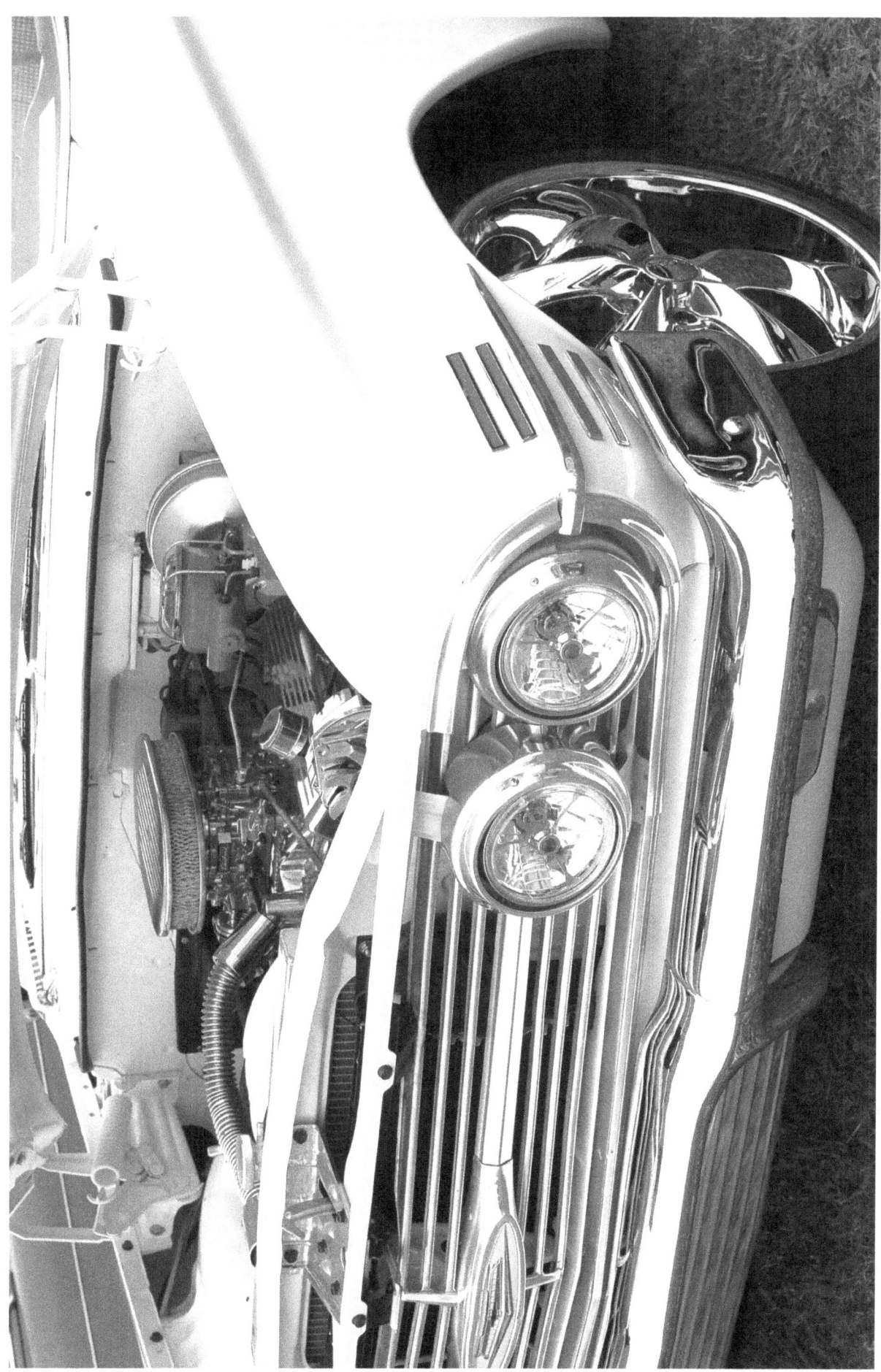

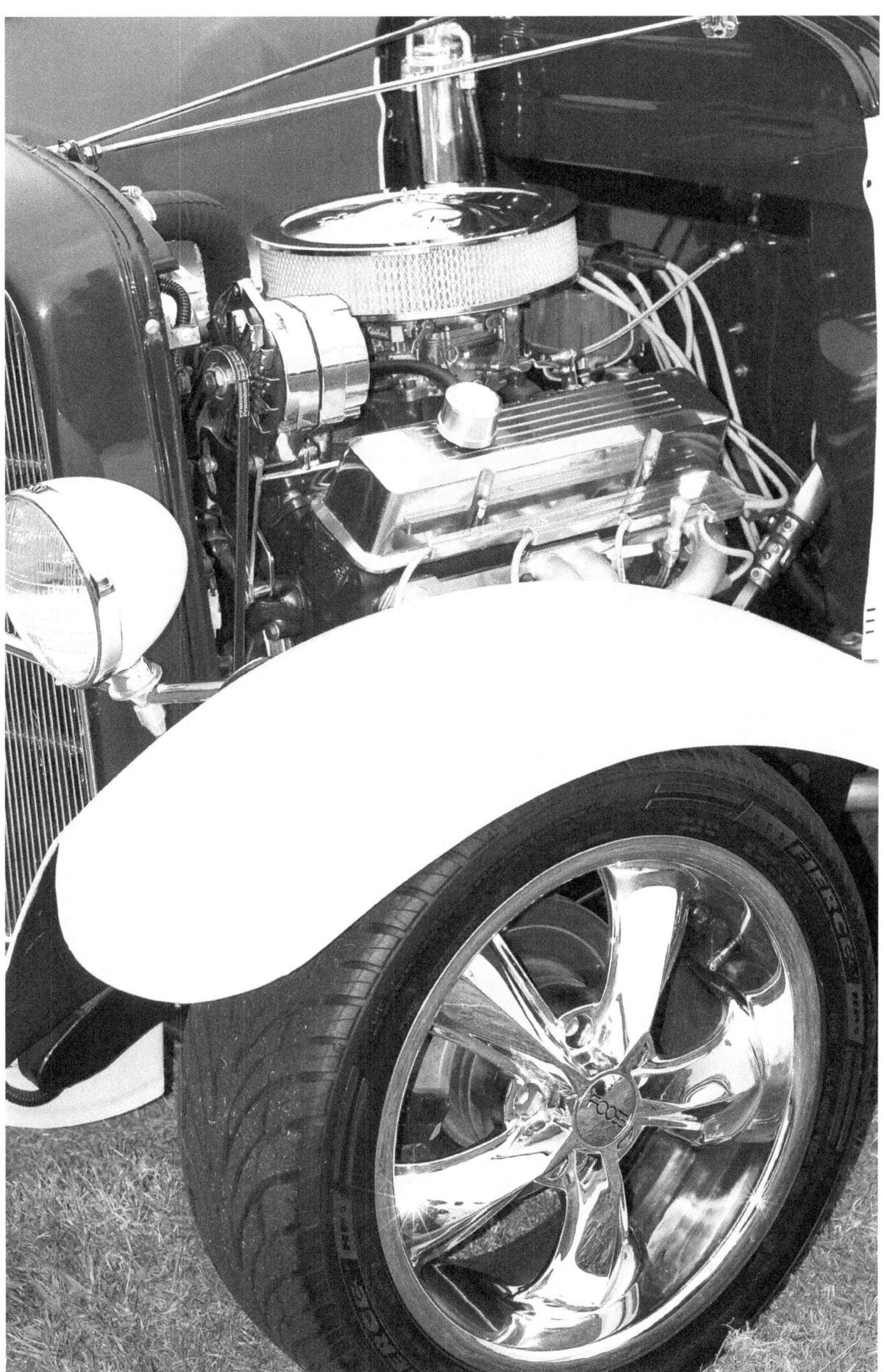

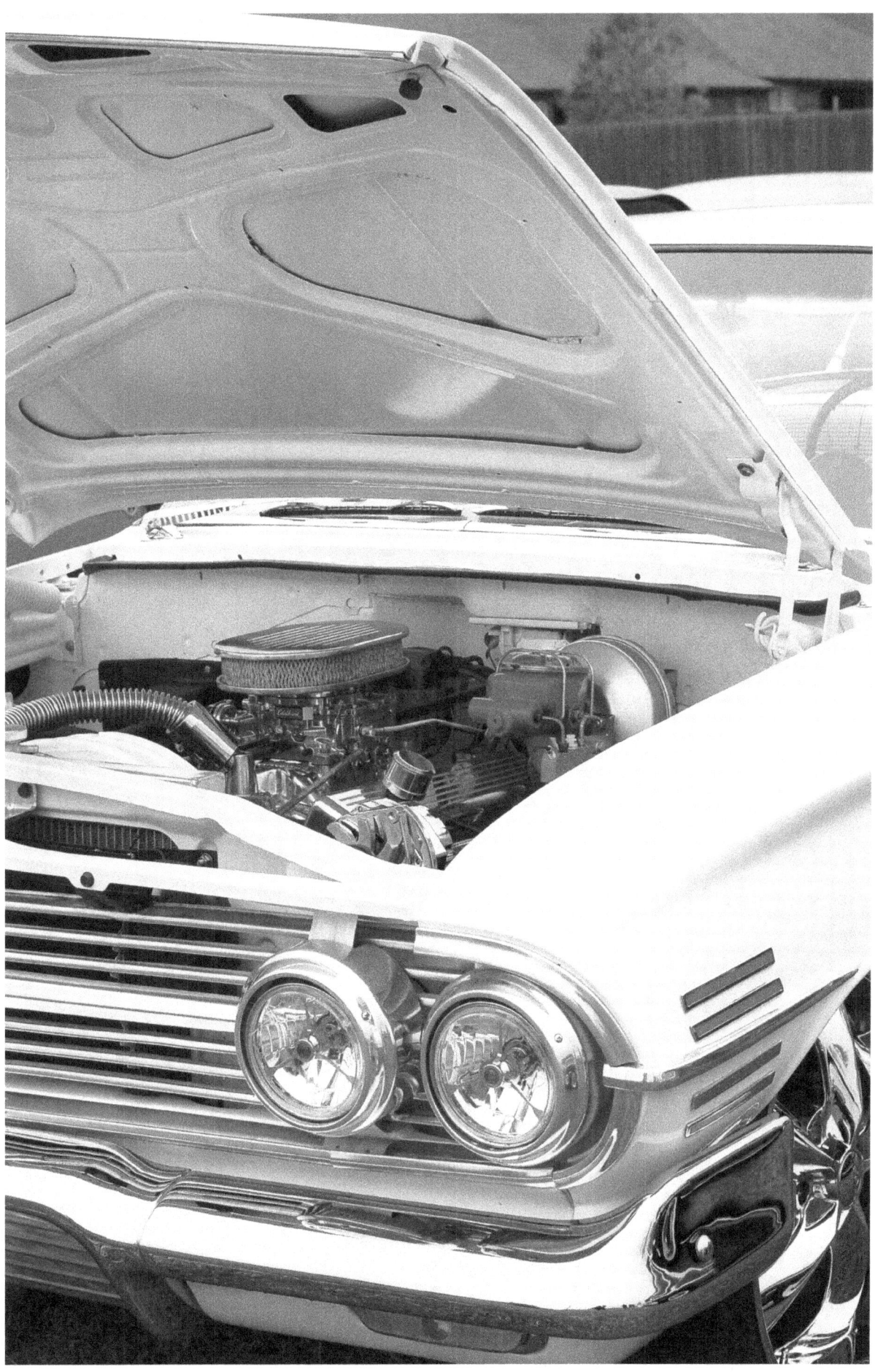

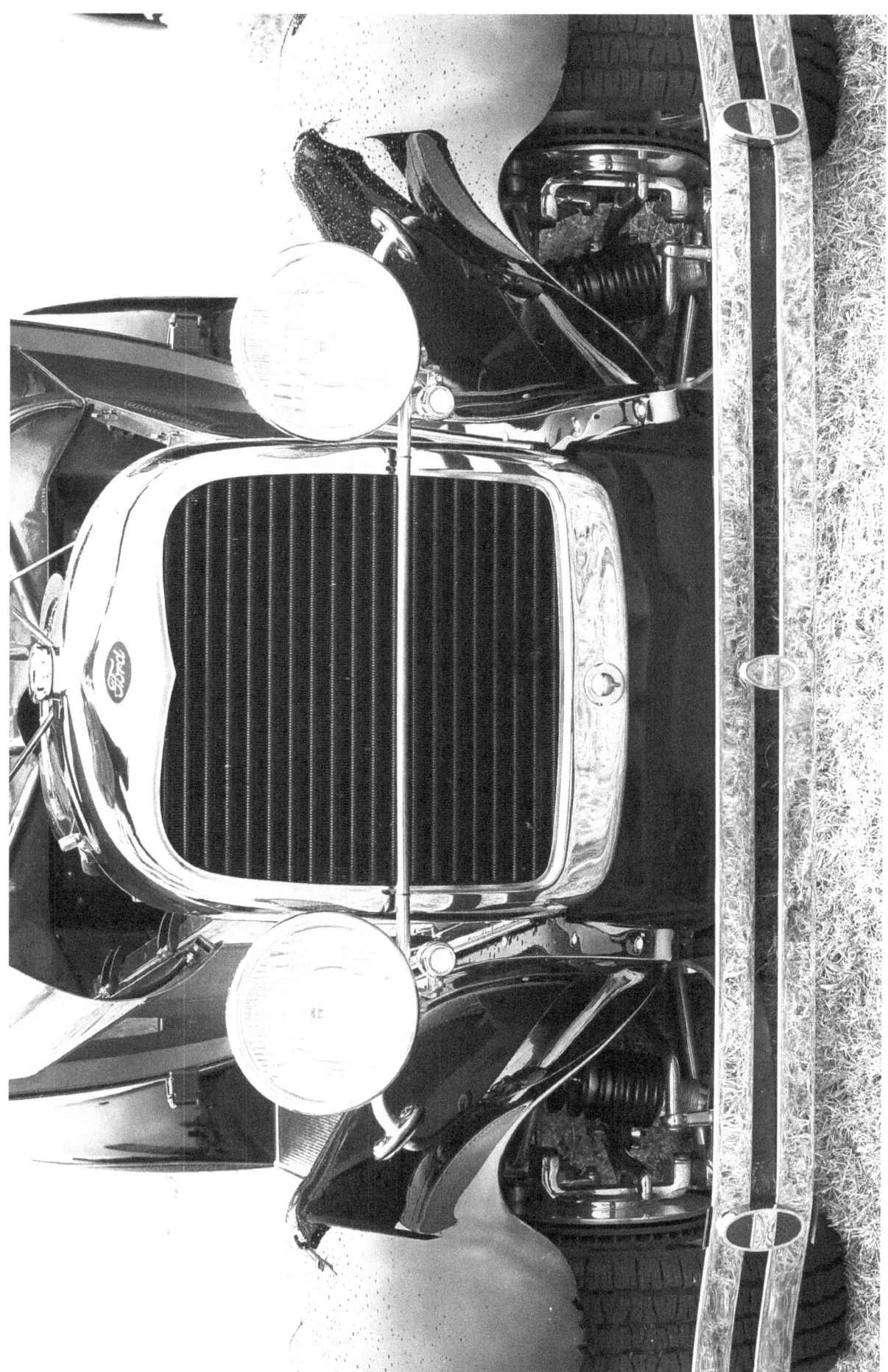

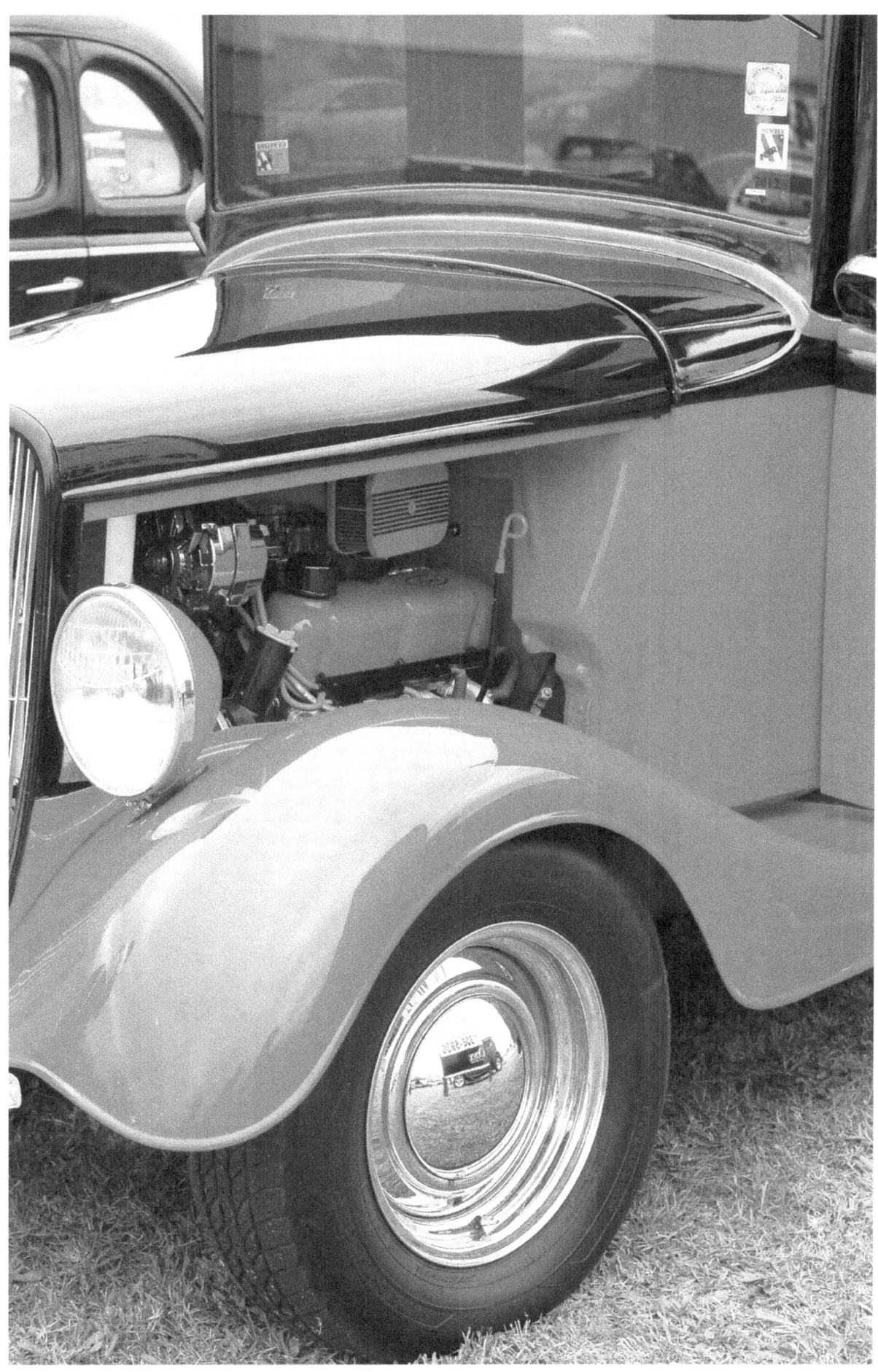

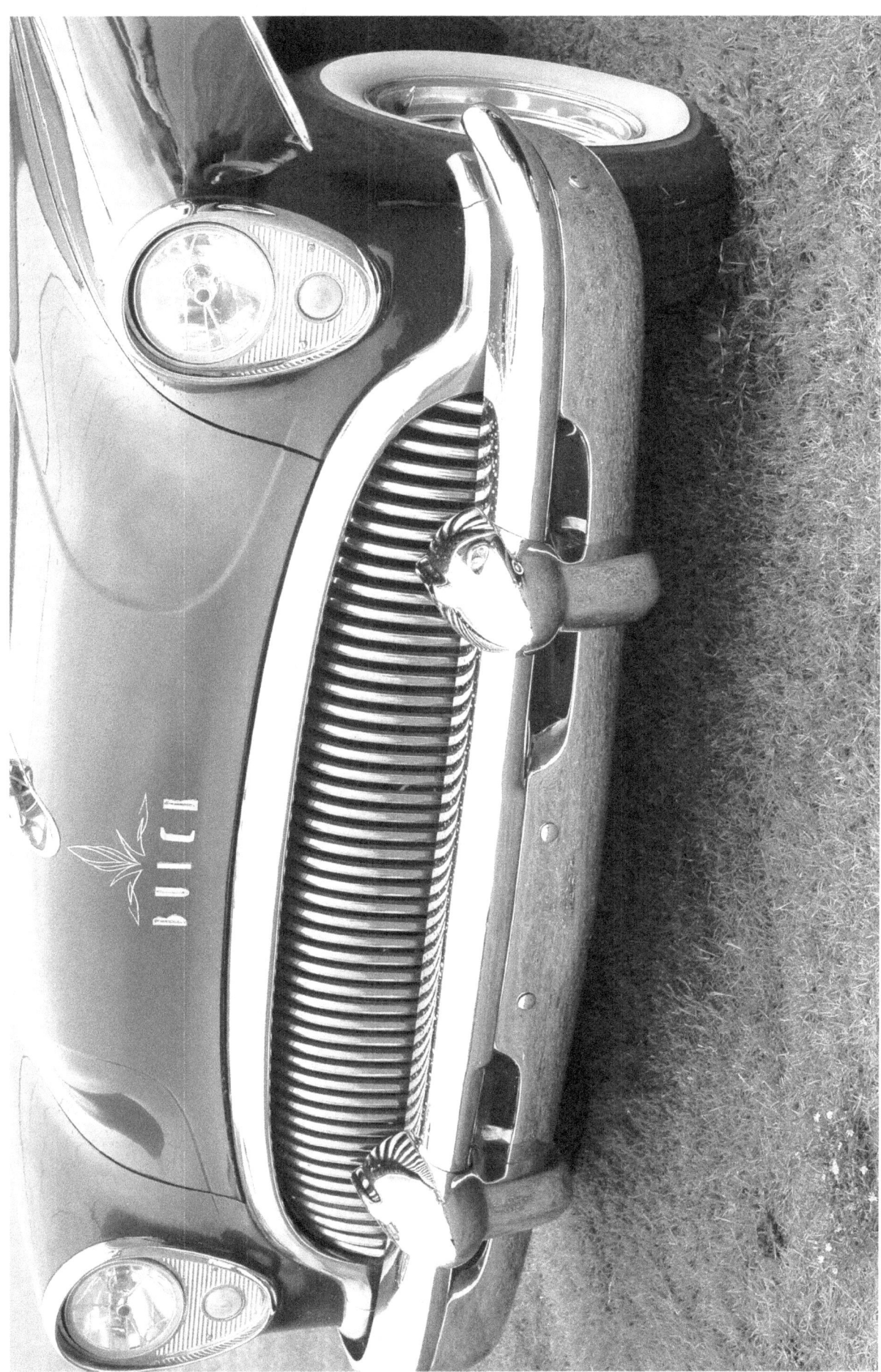

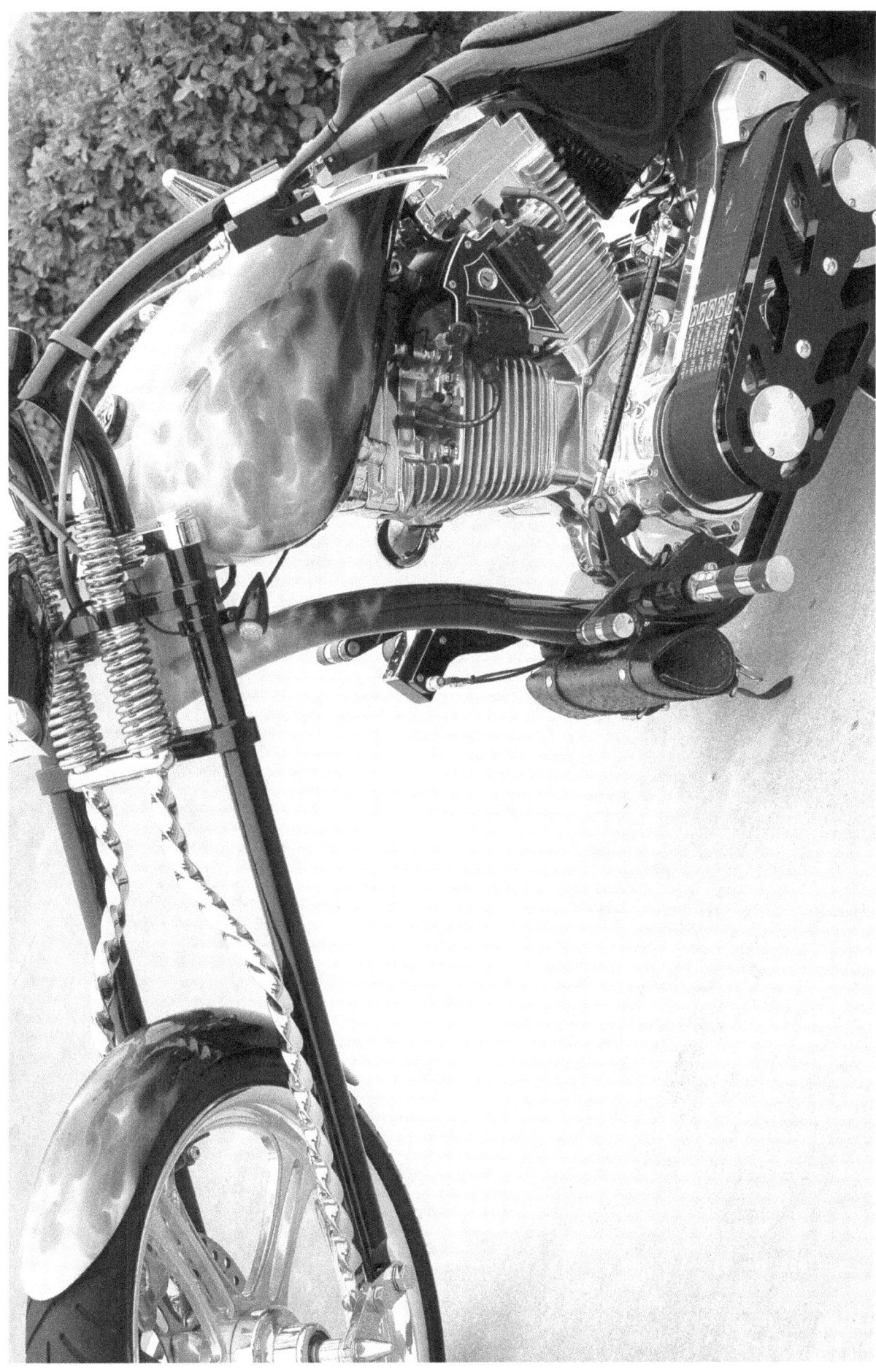

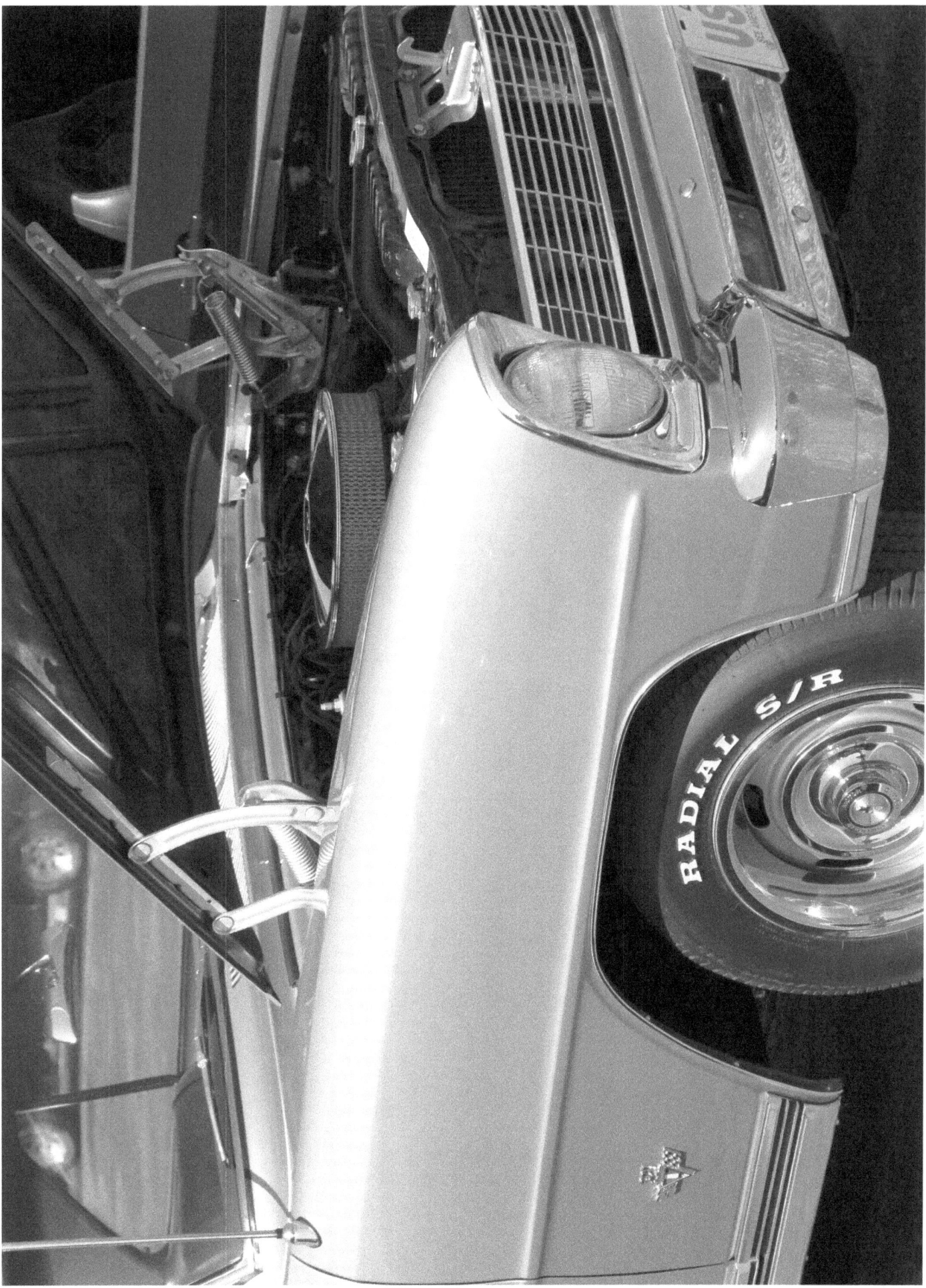

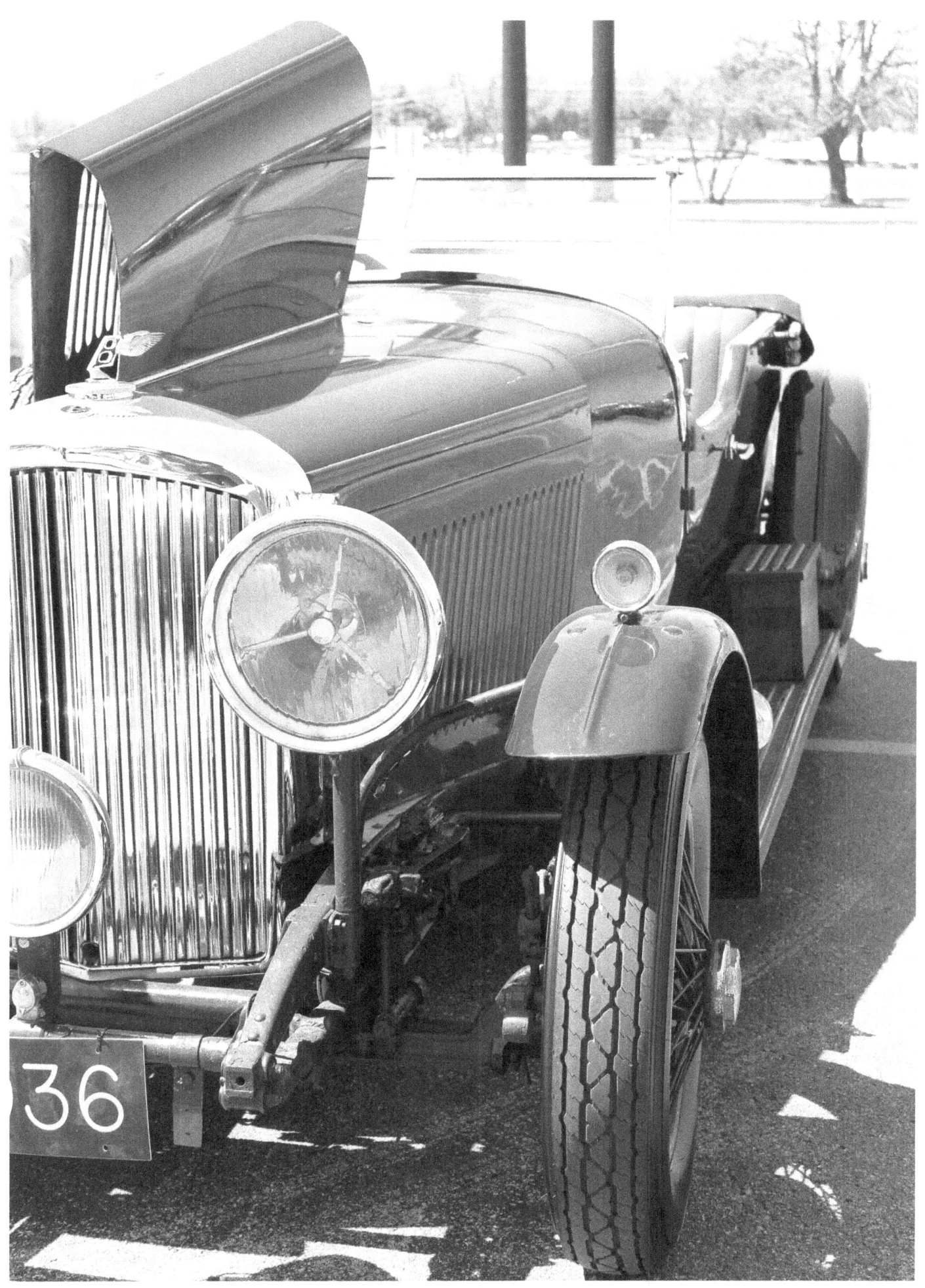

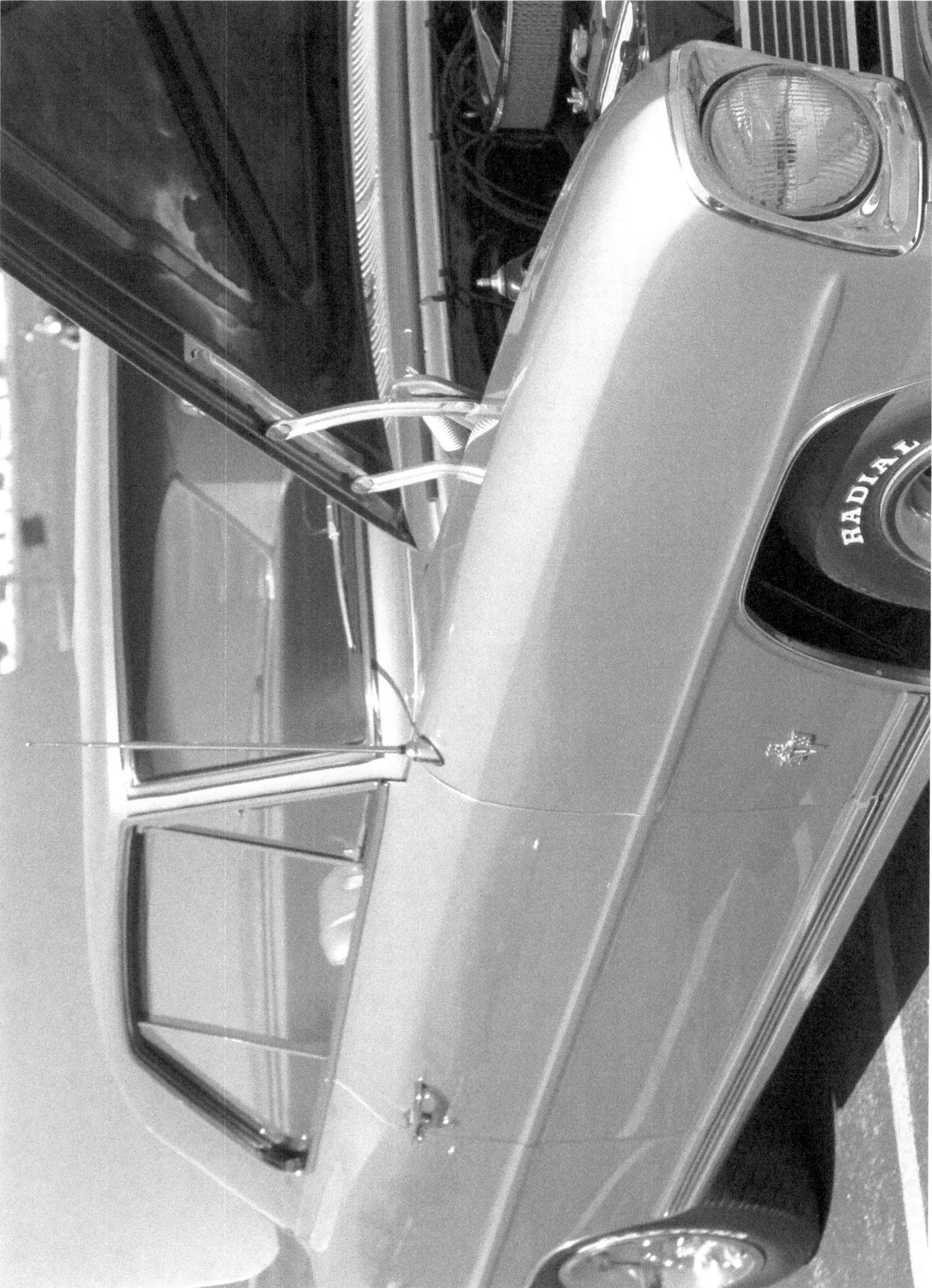

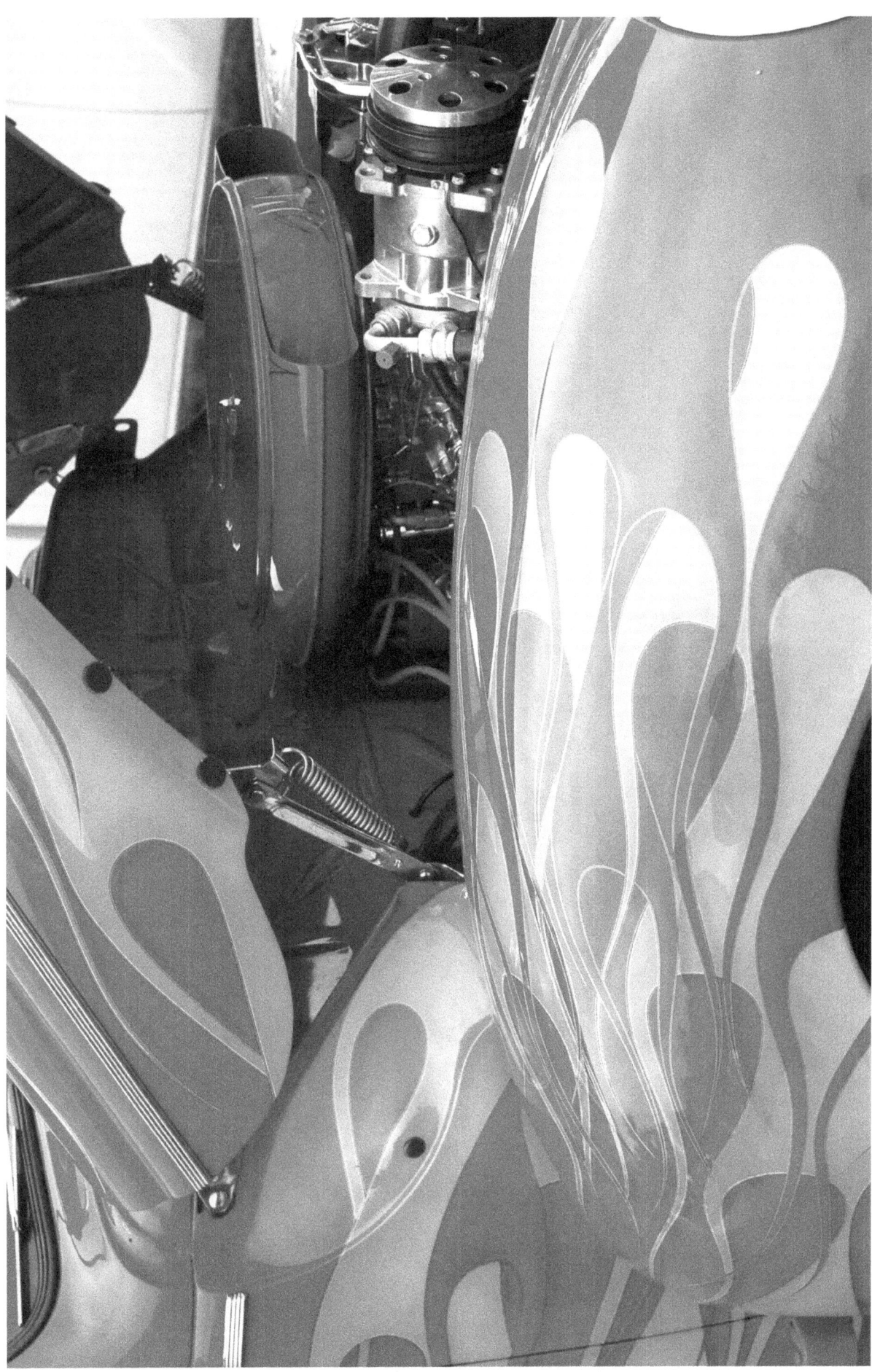

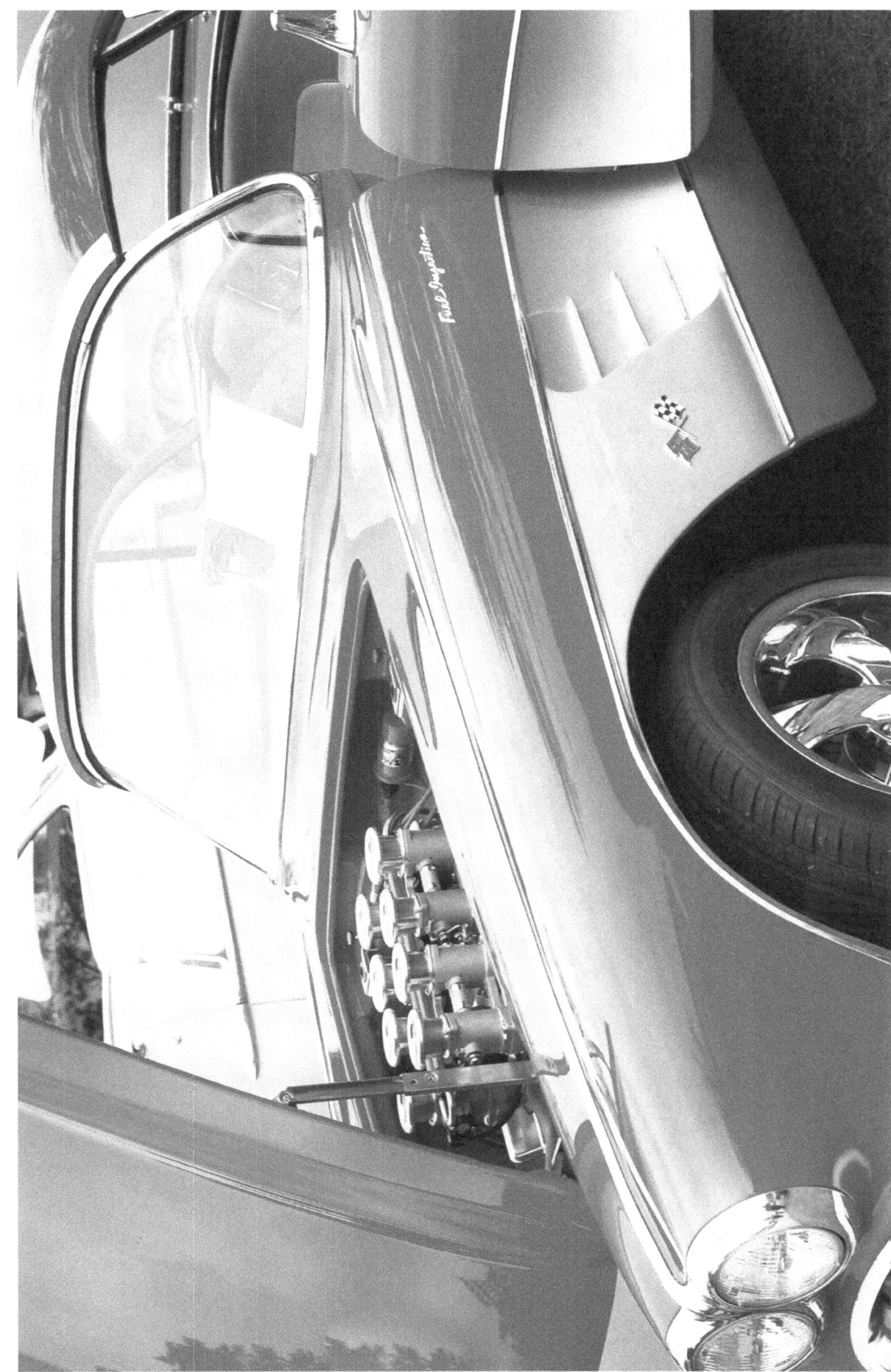

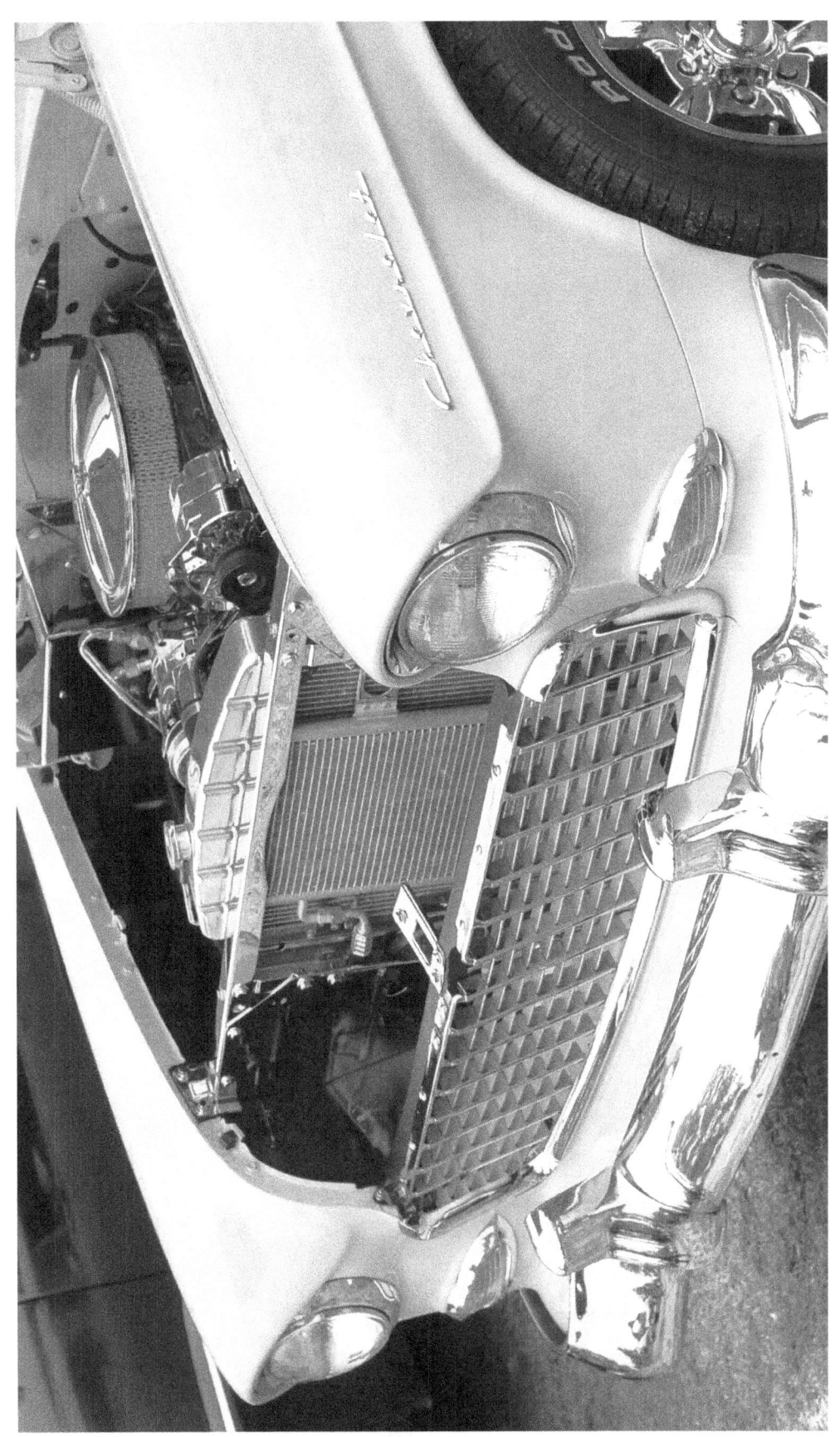

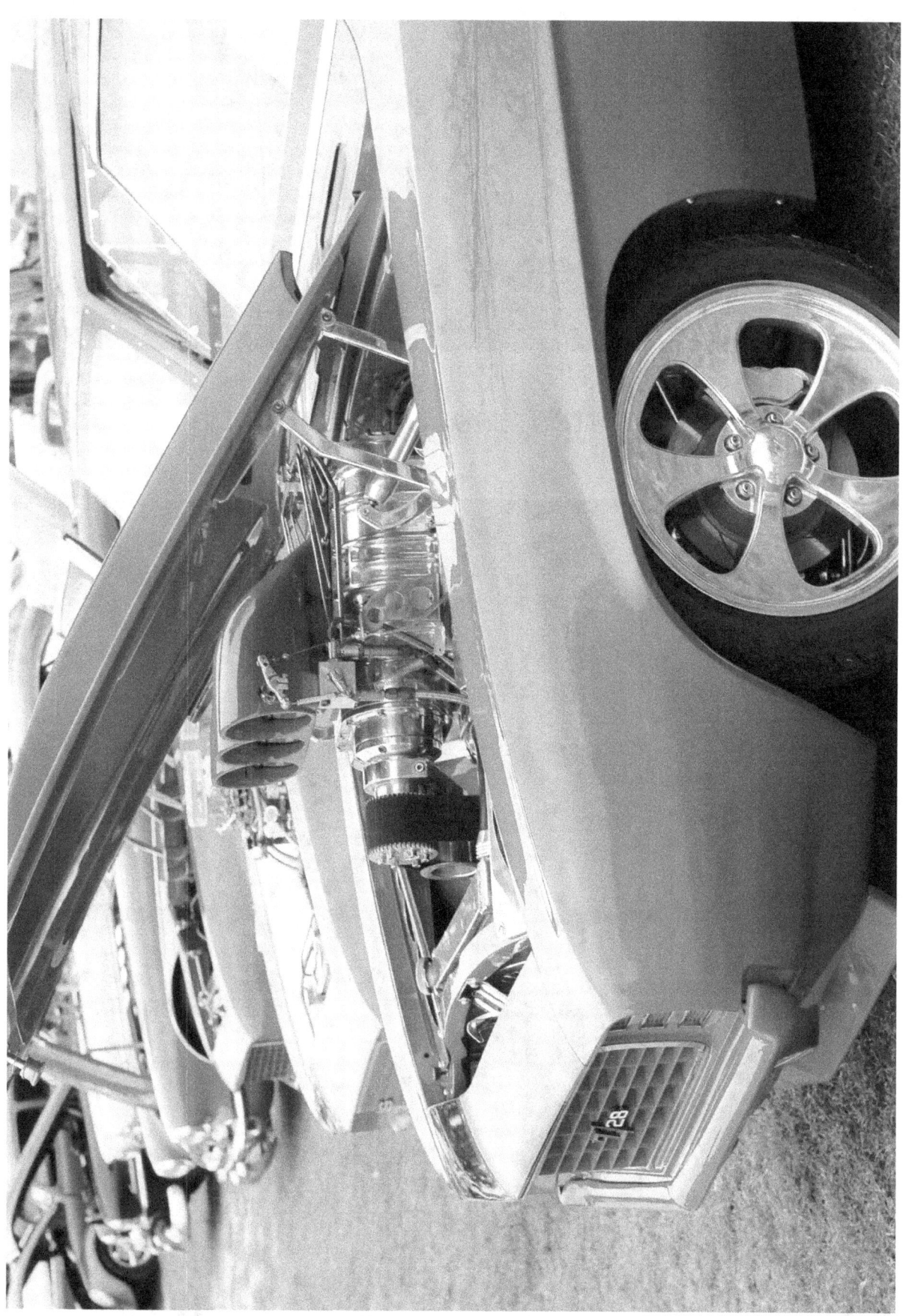

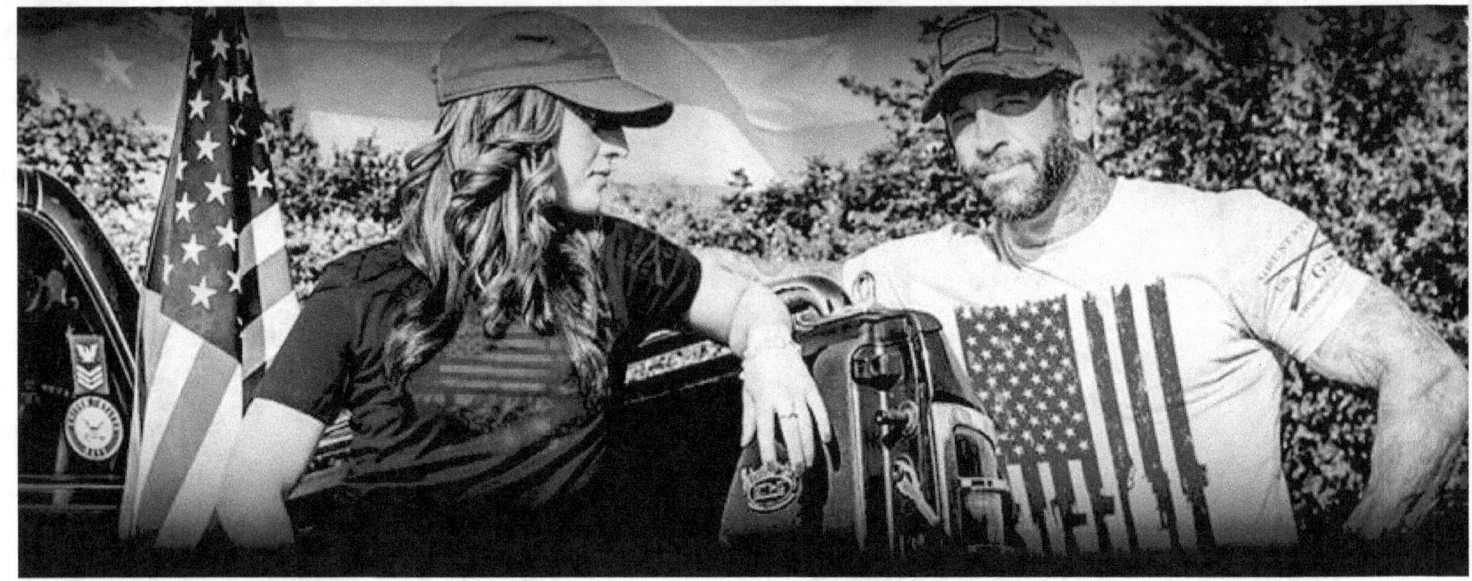

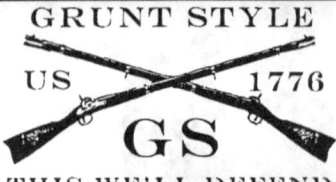

http://mbsy.co/gruntstyle/31536895

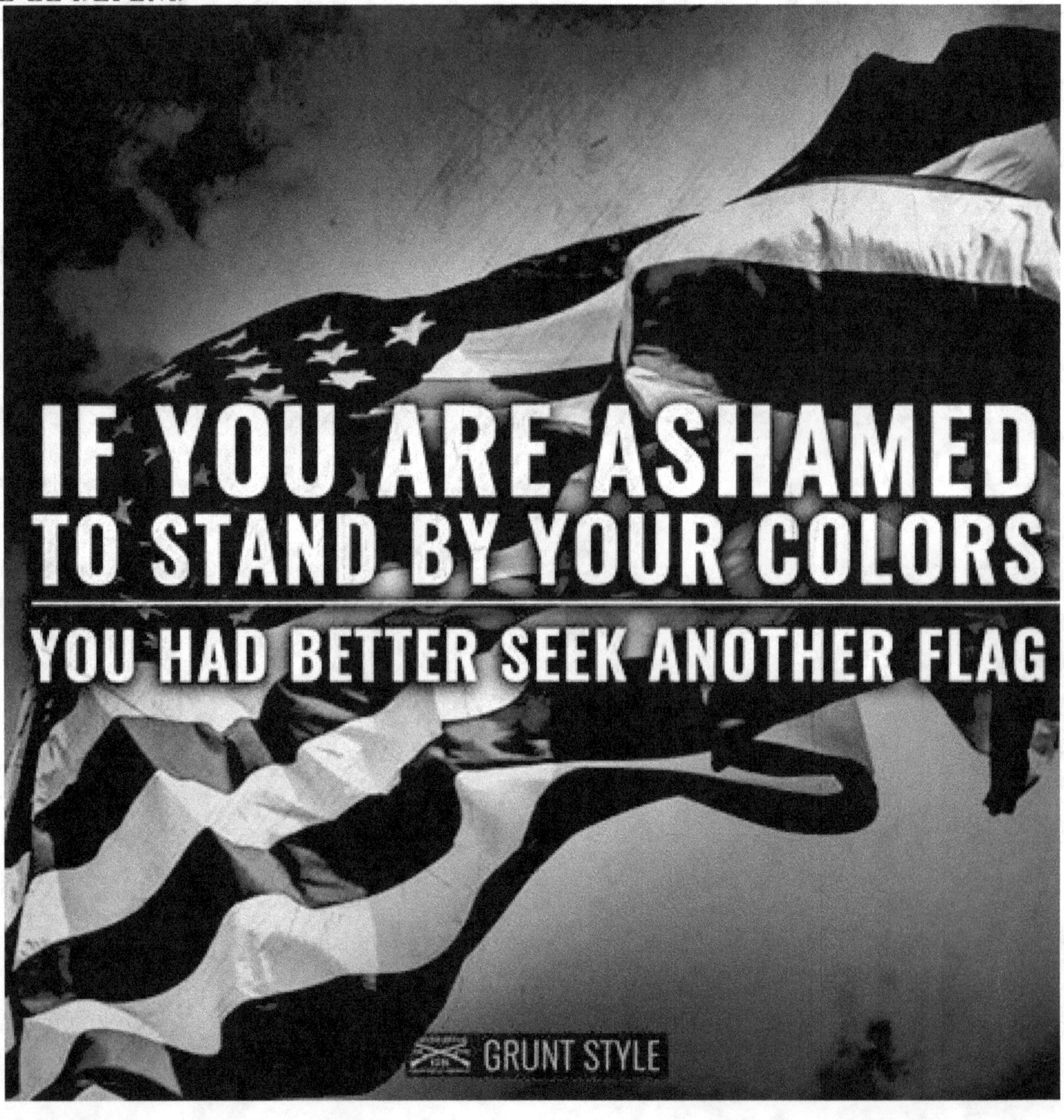

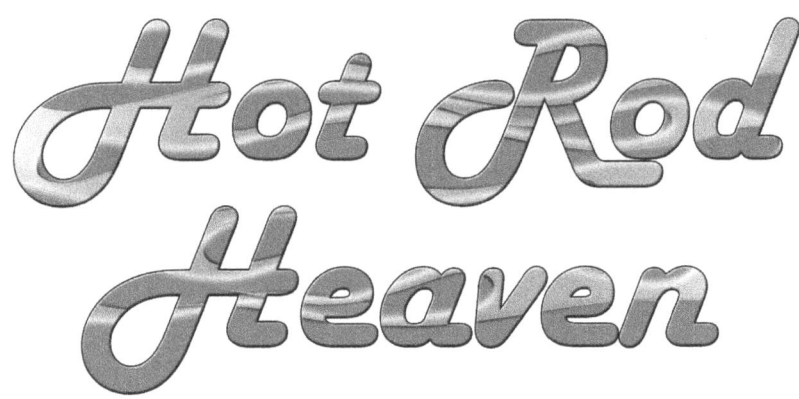

WR Peden is a relatively new author with his very first novella being published on July 1st, 2017. He is a veteran of the United States Marine Corps and has served in Operation Iraqi and Operation Enduring Freedom as well as become a volunteer Fire Fighter for his local community. He is also a current member of the Missouri National Guard and is also a father of 2 girls and a husband to his lovely wife Donna.

Will has been writing since 2000 starting as a teenager writing role-playing scenarios for the electronic wrestling federation's he was a part of. From there he took his imagination to the next level in 2010 opening his own Graphic Design Company. His designs have been seen worldwide from well-known professional wrestling companies in Australia to the internationally known National Wrestling Alliance as the head of Marketing. Will has also done work for the former Indoor Football League team of the Billings Wolves, being the only small business entity working with that team, as well as worked with former WWE/TNA wrestling star and American Ninja Warrior Contestant Zach Gowen and has even has his commercial flyer work published on the back cover of Pro Wrestling Illustrated!

During his time with the National Wrestling Alliance, will picked his passion for writing back up and was not only the designer, producer and layout editor, but he was also an article author for the National Wrestling Alliance Ringside Magazine from 2014-2015 (Available Here). After the magazine closed Will continued writing news stories for several wrestling companies and for the NWA until his departure in late 2015.

In the summer of 2016 Will decided to start the beginning stages of what was to eventually become Book 1 – Soldiers of ZED. Although it has taken over a year to come through, will took every precaution and step to make sure that this novel is successful.

Please visit Hawkstarent.com/wr-peden for the latest information, releases and to sign up for his newsletter!
You can also visit us on Social Media:
Facebook.com/SoldiersofZED
Twitter.com/WRPeden

Tripton-Z Series:
Book 1: Soldiers of ZED
Book 2: Aftermath (Coming Soon)

Adult Grayscale Coloring Books:
Hot Rod Heaven

NWA Ringside Magazine:
September 2014
November 2014
January 2015
Feburary 2015
May 2015

Check out other books by WR Peden online at
www.HawkstarEnt.com/wr-peden